SETS

Spiritually Enlightening Thoughts™

TEACHING CHILDREN HOW TO CONNECT WITH GOD

SHIRLEY HILDRETH

MUSE IMAGERY™

ACKNOWLEDGEMENTS

A special 'thank you' of appreciation to Tom Bird, an exceptional mentor, teacher, and an extraordinary human being without whose guidance this book may never have been written.

Thank you to Manjari Henderson, Louise Crosby, Vincenzo Gagliardi, Dante Corso, for their willingness to share their insights and talents as this book was being born.

A heart full of gratitude to God for inviting me on this most magnificent of journeys.

ABOUT *SETS*

A beautiful, proven method for teaching children about the wonder, gentleness and majesty of God.
Dr. Stephen R. Covey, The 7 Habits of Highly Effective People

This book touches my heart. How wonderful that the author could find such a simple method to help us all make profound differences in life.
Mark Andrews, Emmy Award winning photographer

SETS is an invaluable concept that can encourage our clients to bridge their painful experiences into expressions of hope; and an essential tool for teaching our grandchildren about God, especially the five who are dealing with their gentle mother's lost battle with cancer.
Roberta and Richard Vande Voort, Marriage and Family Therapists

The principles in this wonderful book have opened my eyes to notice more fully the goodness and love of God for all of His children. It is through SETS that I began to be truly grateful, and I feel it a privilege to share this sense of joy and appreciation with others.
Nathan Swain, Student at Mannes College of Music majoring in oboe performance

SETS continue to help me find spiritual depth in every aspect of my life. It is a process that, once started, becomes part of your normal routine, your thought process. You can't ponder on your encounters in life without recognizing a spiritual application.
Kathryn LeMone, English Major, Wife and Mother

I remember the first time that you taught us about SETS and you wanted us to find one during the week and tell you again on Sunday what we had come up with; and I don't think I've stopped since. I realize that God is everywhere and in everything.
Emilee Shelton, Massage Therapist

ABOUT *SETS*

When I think of the symbolism of SETS, I consider the road on which I travel to work each day. It reminds me of the many roads traveled by Jesus on His journey throughout His homeland; roads which He traveled on His way to a destiny prepared by His Father – the same destiny prepared for us.

Dante Corso, President of BC Associated, Inc.

SETS gave me the opportunity to feel my spirit and the spirit of a higher being every day. I found that once I changed my thought process on a spiritual level, I couldn't stop! I am constantly analyzing many items around me and discovering ways to relate them to my spiritual being. I am grateful that I was exposed to such a wonderful way of seeing the world and relating my surroundings to my soul, my heart, and my mind.

Janel Duff, 2nd Grade Teacher

When SETS are a part of every day and every moment, I realize that my days filled with feeding, clothing and bathing a child are all spiritual practices; I simply have to choose to make them such.

Amanda Suarez, Full time student, full time mother, and part time massage therapist

I am now married with two children, and I am teaching the young women in my church. I have introduced SETS to my class and enjoy watching them grow each week as they become more in tune with God. I am also excited to teach my children to find SETS in all of their surroundings, as it will help them to recognize their divine nature and the tremendous love God has for them.

Jennie Slade, A wife to her best friend Chad, mother of Taylor and Jackson

SETS enhance life and by connecting with God they assist you in finding and knowing what you were born to do. I'm not talking about your job in the world, but the job for you. They invite you to spend the energy in the "I can" rather than "I can't". SETS are tools for success.

Bryce Krausman, President/Founder of Food Snobs.com

To my children, Andrea, Troy, and Kerri, and my cousin Stuart in appreciation of their love, understanding, and support.

And to those young women whom I taught who valiantly continue to practice today, those lessons learned in class so many years ago.

SETS
Spiritually Enlightening Thoughts™

TEACHING CHILDREN HOW TO CONNECT WITH GOD

SHIRLEY HILDRETH

MUSE IMAGERY™

SETS
Spiritually Enlightening Thoughts™
TEACHING CHILDREN HOW TO CONNECT WITH GOD

TABLE OF CONTENTS

INTRODUCTION

This book is about a teaching method called **S**piritually **E**nlightening **T**hought**s** (**SETS**)™. It builds on the premise that thoughts precede actions and that God-based thoughts bring about God-based actions. It invites you, the reader, to take a spiritual journey and MAKE TIME FOR GOD by reprioritizing your life and connecting or reconnecting, whichever the case may be, with Him.

This book then invites you to share what you have learned with the children in your charge. It explains that you must begin with yourself before you can teach another and gives you the tools to be able to do so.

HOW TO USE THIS BOOK

1. Read PART I that talks about this 21st - century world in which we live and explains what SETS are. This part of the book also contains profound testimonials of young women who were taught the SETS Method and are now, over eight years later, not only <u>still practicing</u> SETS, but are teaching SETS to their own children as well as others. These writings demonstrate that SETS have proven to be **long-lasting** and **life-changing**.

2. Read PART II that invites you to step into a child's world and helps you to understand that <u>each</u> child, and the child that lives within all of us, has gifts of the Spirit that were endowed by God; and that <u>each</u> of us, no matter what our circumstances, has divine potential. It explains that as we connect with God, become aware of our gifts, and develop them in His way, we will begin our magnificent journey along the path that leads us back to Him.

3. Read PART III and begin with yourself by connecting the child within you to God. It invites you to practice the SETS Method in your own life before you begin to teach another and includes the <u>SETS Method for the INDIVIDUAL</u> that will enable you to accomplish this.

4. PART IV encourages you to teach what you have learned and provides helpful instructions for you as you prepare to teach the SETS Method.

Determine whom you will be teaching. Will it be in a classroom or family setting? Then read to understand the SETS Method teaching module in PART IV that applies. Now begin to teach the most important lesson you will ever teach – *Teaching Children How To Connect With God.*

5. **Let me hear from you!**

PART V asks you to practice the SETS Method for a minimum of three (3) months for the INDIVIDUAL or six (6) months in a FAMILY or CLASSROOM setting. It then invites you to let me hear from you by going to my website at www.SETSconnection.com and share your faith-promoting SETS experiences for possible inclusion in future books that are right now on the 'drawing board.' The two categories we are looking for are:

 a. Profound examples of faith-promoting SETS.

   and

 b. How practicing the SETS Method has changed your life and/or the lives of those you have taught.

If your experience is chosen, it may be included in future books that will incorporate individual, personal experiences of those who have practiced and/or taught the SETS Method.

6. Keep a record of your own SETS on the journal pages in PART VI.

PART I

IN QUEST OF 'SETS'

"Ask, and it shall be given you; seek, and ye shall find; knock, and it shall be opened unto you. For every one that asketh receiveth; and he that seeketh findeth; and to him that knocketh, it shall be opened."

Sermon on the Mount – St. Matthew 7:7, 8

"I am not bound to win, but
I am bound to be true.
I am not bound to succeed, but
I am bound to live up to what light I have."
Abraham Lincoln

CHAPTER 1

A WAKE-UP CALL — REALITY CHECK — THE PRICE OF AFFLUENCE

Contained within the magic of our souls is a gentle longing for home, placed there by our Creator to act as a needle on a compass giving us direction on our journey. The great deceiver would have us believe that those longings can be satisfied by the things of this world. They cannot.

There are nearly 72,000,000 children under the age of 18 in the United States. Many books have been written about how to 'fix' a child after he or she has gone wrong; to deal, after the fact, with the problems of childhood. Few books have been written to explain, in simple terms, how to teach children to connect with God, the ultimate cure for all of our ills. From birth this is a gift that is innate in the child, but one that may have been taken away from the child and is often overlooked in the nurturing process.

As we look upon the world in which we live, what do we see? It is a world of ever-changing values. A world where children are sometimes given little consideration as their parents hurl themselves toward selfish desires. It is a world of great uncertainty, a confusing world for a child. A world of contradictions. A world where people say I love you, then in stark reality, act the opposite. A world with uncertainty about the future. A world in which the child now asks not only why 9-11 happened, but when will it happen again? A world where information and technology is moving nearly too fast to keep up with. Does time seem to be rushing ahead of their footsteps? Has the security children once experienced been replaced with fear and doubt?

As I have been preparing to write this book I took the occasion to visit local bookstores to research the works already published relative to the subject matter I was writing about. Two of the large chain-type bookstores had a magnificent array of books on every subject you can imagine. They were so well stocked they seemed like huge retail 'libraries.' I checked the shelves on religion, child psychology, and in the children's section of the self-help books. Nothing! This can't be! Perhaps I needed to check out the religious bookstores. I went to one that was non-denominational and one bookstore of a specific religion and to my amazement again, nothing.

Another interesting fact I observed in my journey through the bookstores: there are shelves upon shelves of self-help books for adults, telling us how to live our lives, defeat our self-defeating behaviors, heal the inner child, and overcome depression. There are also many books, however fewer than the adult buffet of self-help, about children and how to deal with ADHD (attention deficit hyperactivity disorder); how to practice tough love with a rebellious teen; childhood depression and how to deal with it; drug and alcohol abuse and your teen; anger in children. These books for and about children are all in-depth books explaining how to deal with children <u>after</u> they have taken that first wrong step. <u>After</u> they are hooked on the negative actions that got them to that point.

Why not a book to give the child a solid foundation for all things good and wonderful there are in this world. Why not give them their own spiritual taste of the divinity of God?

Judging by the number of books for the grand array of adult neuroses, we seem to be looking for answers that focus on us. We are reading profusely about, and searching for answers to what we perceive as our most perplexing 21st - century questions. These are questions about how to 'fix' ourselves. We then sidestep asking and run from finding the answer to the question, "How do we avoid having to find a 'fix'?"

How much time do we spend searching for some cure, some help in this array of perceived ailments and neuroses served up on the shelves? We seem to be so caught up with self that we forget about God and how connecting with Him and developing a relationship with Him will give us the needed aid we so desperately seek. The answer is simple, but we do not ask. We are looking in the wrong places. He has presented the answers to our most complex, irresolvable problems and we do not seek.

In *Mere Christianity*, C. S. Lewis provides the following insights, "Now God designed the human machine to run on Himself. He Himself is the fuel our spirits were designed to burn, or the food our spirits were designed to feed on." He also says that as people we are many times, "trying to run on the wrong juice." He further talks about something evading us and "when the real want for Heaven is present in us, we do not recognize it. Most people if they had really learned to look into their own hearts, would know that what they do want, and want acutely, is something that cannot be had in this world."

So many times we look for things outside of Him to bring us happiness and joy. That type of joy is temporary and fleeting. Lasting but a short time then sending us out, once again, in a new search for that illusive something that will quench a thirst that we have wrongly defined. We have presumed that what the world tells us will bring us joy is correct, i.e., money, power, authority, material things; but all the time true joy lives within our ability to connect with God. To see things as He would have us see them and to recognize His hand in all things. To see, feel, touch, experience His creations in the palm of our hand and be grateful for them all.

St. Matthew 7:7, 8 reads, "Ask, and it shall be given you; seek, and ye shall find; knock, and it shall be opened unto you. For everyone that asketh receiveth; and he that seeketh findeth; and to him that knocketh, it shall be opened." All we have to do is look beyond ourselves, look to Him and ask, seek, knock. It's that simple.

Spirituality is like medicine, and to heal the illness it is not enough to look at the medicine and talk about it, you have to ingest it. And so it is with the goodness in life. You have to ingest it. There are shelves full of remedies, the world explains, that will cure your ills. A close connection with God should be the first prescription written, the first medicine taken before all else.

This time of our existence on earth is treacherous with many conflicting voices pulling us in varied directions. The voices seem to be getting louder as blatant evils move closer to our families and our individual selves. At this time there is also a very evident amount of goodness in this world, seemingly in counter-balance to the evil that prevails. Good people seem to be seeking each other out, and becoming more firm in their stance for good. It is becoming easier to differentiate between good and evil, as the distance is greater and very apparent.

If we were to use a graphic to illustrate the condition of our world, some would suggest that at this time of our mortal existence the balance beam would look a lot like this:

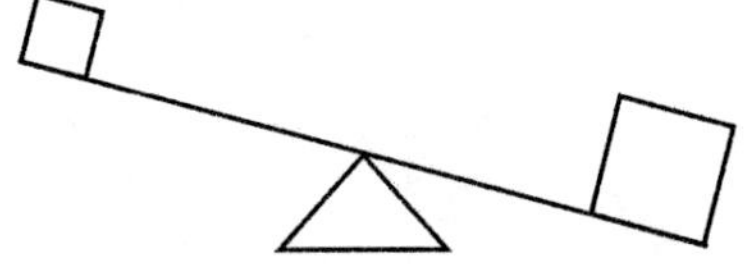

With evil weighing more heavily than good, the emphasis must be placed on neutralizing the negative side by a) adding more weight to the positive side, or b) moving the fulcrum (the pivotal point or center) toward God, thereby balancing the beam.

Do you remember, as a child, playing on the seesaw? Certainly the heaviest one would have the edge and the lightest one with less substance, would find themselves high in the air with nowhere to turn and at the mercy of the heavier one. The **Spiritually Enlightening Thoughts (SETS)** Method taught in this book, when practiced, will add substance to all that is positive in life. It will bring the life of the student as well as the teacher back into harmony and balance once again.

Last summer I bought a blue iridescent gazing ball for my back yard. It distorts the image but is fun to look at. As long as we <u>know reality,</u> we won't be fooled by a distorted image.

We live in a very fast-paced world. A world that seems to bombard us with so much stimulation, both visual and auditory, that it keeps our focus from the real world around us. There is a false substitute world of rush, hurry, worry, and anxiety – pushing and nagging us into moving faster, working faster, thinking faster. This becomes the perfect haven for all of those who want to escape from themselves; for those who for one reason or another are afraid to be alone with themselves and their own thoughts. They can push, drive, and flog themselves into submission with a multitude of daily tasks. Yes, it is essential that we focus because that's what gets things done. But consider the executive who is so focused on the bottom line that he justifies dishonest actions and excludes the peripheral nuances, namely honesty, along the way. He has the wrong focus. Oh, it's fine to be able to focus and thus achieve. But it is also important that the focus, the prescription in the lens through which we view life, is the correctly ground prescription for our eyes. If a nearsighted person places a farsighted person's glasses on the bridge of their nose, they won't be able to see clearly. The world around them will become confused, blurred and fuzzy. Not that the world is blurred and fuzzy, but it is the lens through which the observer looks that determines their reality – their clarity of vision.

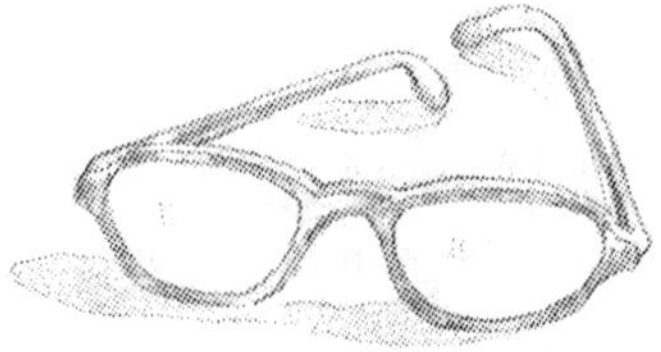

What is your reality? It is all predicated upon your perceptions about life, and your perceptions are based on your focus and how you view life. If you could change that view, that perception, your entire life would be changed. By re-focusing on the reality around you and looking at life through the lens of gratefulness and love you are able to see the gifts of the spirit and God's love that surround you. It's all about slowing down, changing focus to look for a spiritual meaning and purpose to life, and when you do this you will begin to recognize that all things testify to this end.

A few years ago Stephen E. Robinson wrote a thought-provoking book entitled *Believing Christ*, in which he explains, "If we only believe in Christ without believing Christ, then we are like people sitting in cold, dark houses surrounded by unused lamps and heaters, people who believe in electricity but who never threw the switch to turn on the power. Though the appliances may all work and the wiring may be in good order, until we accept the power itself, beyond merely believing in the theory of power, we cannot enjoy the warmth and the light."

I invite you to join with me as we learn how to teach not only the children but ourselves to connect with the power of God by 'throwing the switch' and entering into His warmth and light.

AND HE SAID, "FOLLOW ME…LEARN OF ME…DO WHAT YOU HAVE SEEN ME DO…

I AM THE WAY…THE TRUTH…THE LIGHT."

(St. Matthew 11:29, 16:24; St. John 9:5, 14:16; Judges 9:48)

"Never loose an opportunity of seeing anything that is beautiful:
for beauty is God's handwriting – a wayside sacrament.
Welcome it in every fair face, in every fair sky, in every fair flower,
And thank God for it as a cup of blessing."
Ralph Waldo Emerson

CHAPTER 2

UNDERSTANDING WHAT SETS ARE

All it takes to see a miracle are the eyes of faith.

I would invite you to ask yourself the following questions: "If you could teach a child but one lesson, the most valuable lesson in the world, what would it be?" "What could you teach that would provide nourishment to the spirit, comfort from the chill winds of adversity, hope in the future, and an understanding to the child that they are loved by God, unconditionally?" I would offer this to you: that if you could teach a child how to connect with God, to tune in to His spirit, to feel His unconditional love for them, it would not only be the most valuable lesson you could teach but the greatest gift you could give. By learning this one principle, building upon it and having it as the strength and foundation in the child's life, all of the remaining life experiences will fall into place and be built upon the rock of His love.

It is important for you to also understand as you read this book that as we talk of teaching children, you are the teacher and caregiver of the child that lies deep within your soul; the child who longs to be heard and understood; the child who is fervently reaching out to be taught to connect with God and feel the unconditional love and acceptance that only He can give.

The core idea of this book is to teach children, and the child that lies within each of us, to have

Spiritually Enlightening Thoughts (SETS) on a continual basis by becoming aware of the world around us and recognizing His hand in all things. This process results in a close, long-lasting connection to God.

SETS builds on the premise that thoughts precede actions. If we can guide thought in a positive direction by making spiritual associations, the actions will follow accordingly. It is about re-focusing on those things spiritual. When we can see life through the lens of the spirit, we can see forever. James Allen quotes these timely words in his book, *As A Man Thinketh*, "As a man thinketh, so is he, and as he continues to think, so he remains." He also tells us that "all that we are is a result of what we have thought." And so it is with a child. By teaching children to think spiritually enlightening thoughts, you are facilitating their quest to connect with their Creator, and in so doing build a bright future on the foundation of His love.

As children, we were curious and marveled at the wonders of this earthly existence. We were always exploring, looking for answers. Then, as we grew and matured, we lost most of that innocent trust and believing and our focus was placed more on the material world in which we live. This book re-kindles the flame that lies buried within each of us. It lights the fire of the knowledge of who we are and what our purpose on earth is all about. When the lessons from this book are taught to a child, both the teacher and the student will have an experience personal to each as they seek to find a connection to God within its pages. It does not matter what religion the reader may be for the concepts taught in this book are at the heart of all religions that believe there is a God.

St. Matthew 7:7 ~ "Ask, and it shall be given you; seek and ye shall find; knock, and it shall be opened unto you." Together we are going to "ask," "seek," and "knock."

The idea is simple. By using the SETS Method outlined in this book, the child will be taught to connect a spiritual thought with everyday natural objects such as flowers, leaves, stones, and twigs, etc. For example, for the *flower*, the beauty of God is all around us; for the *leaf*, the leaf uses the energy of the sun (light) to make nutrients for the tree. We also use the energy of the Son to nourish our soul; for the *stone*, our testimony of God is strong like the stone; for the *twig*, straight is the path back to God.

As children become aware of their surroundings, they begin to see with their spiritual eyes the signposts God has placed for all of us along the way, and they will begin to feel God's unconditional love for them. Observing natural beauty helps children understand that all things on earth, if observed and contemplated, can testify to a spiritual end. As children develop their ability to recognize God's hand in all things, they begin to see divinity in the world around them and their actions follow accordingly.

As teaching the concept of SETS evolves over time, the objects chosen may become more material such as an eraser, a glass of water, a match, a 'stop sign' along the highway, or anything else the child may think of. For example, for the *eraser*, God can erase away our sins and He remembers them no more. For the *glass of water*, God is the living water of life. For the *match*, He will light our way in the darkness. For the *stop sign*, it is important to stop and think before we do things.

Thich Nhat Han, in his bestselling book, *Peace Is Every Step*, tells us that "when we are capable of stopping, we begin to see, and if we can see, we can understand."

Let me give you an example of how, if we are aware, we can relate a SET to even the most seemingly technical of every day experiences.

Sometimes we make life too complicated when all we have to do to connect with God is jiggle the cord.

At my office, since a new department had just been formed, our Information Services Department was moving the computer programs from one server to another. With trembling, we turned the computers off on Friday and had our fingers crossed that on Monday, when we turned them back on, they would work.

Monday I got to the office and the software seemed okay, except for an interface with a color printer. Of course, I always felt like the printer was on a power trip and would print when it was 'darn good and ready.' Tuesday it was even worse. Then, I found that there was something very wrong with my monitor. Looked like it had blown the video card. I was missing the color 'red.' Although living in a blue and green world wouldn't be all that bad, it was very hard on the eyes. I called tech support who immediately, within four or five hours, came to my aid. They reinstalled the drivers and decided it was either the video card or I needed a new monitor, and they would have to invite tech support, one hierarchy level up from them, to fix it. My friendship with the bottle of Visine® grew daily. Then, one of my co-workers came to my desk, got down on his hands and knees and jiggled the monitor cord. Voila! It was fixed. All that was needed to fix what had been diagnosed as a monitor problem of major proportions was to jiggle the cord. A simple, lasting fix and one that took care of the problem. Tech support had assumed some gigantic problem and had overlooked the simple answer.

In life we sometimes try to remedy the ills of the world, assuming some gigantic problem, when the answer is very simple. An answer often overlooked as we seek to weave the more complex notions of life into our lives, thinking that in complexity lies success and joy. The **S**piritually **E**nlightening **T**hought**s** (SETS) Method shared in this book is simple. It's like jiggling the cord so that the connection to God can become clear and vibrant. It enables the child, and the child within each of us, to see our world in vivid hues of color.

It is that simple.

The <u>ultimate goal</u> in the entire SETS teaching process is to bring the one being taught to a point of full awareness so that they will begin to have spiritually enlightening thoughts and make the connection with God on their own apart from the associations that are presented by the teacher. When they can accomplish this task, they will have begun a wonderful journey of peace, love, and acceptance with God as their guide. They will begin to see who they are and how they fit into this mosaic we call mortal life.

This teaching method invites the teacher to begin with himself or herself. It asks that the teacher prayerfully practice having SETS and invite God to be their partner in the teaching process. It explains that children need to feel the teacher's enthusiasm and passion for what they are teaching before they will believe in the process.

Intermittently over the past 20 years, I have taught the young people in our church. One such group of young women, whose ages ranged between 14 and 16 years old, were in my class for two years beginning nearly ten years ago. We had well-written lesson manuals and wonderful visual aids for the classroom, but I felt I was not providing a strong enough foundation to assist them in reaching deep into their spiritual core to provide a long-lasting connection with God that would guide them throughout their life.

I pondered and prayed and asked God to help me find a way to create a closer link between the girls and Him. I needed to find a way to teach them to 'tune in to God.' It was out of these prayers that the concept of teaching **S**piritually **E**nlightening **T**hought**s** (SETS) was born.

I now realize, over eight years later, that the SETS Method of learning is long-lasting. It is a concept that has stayed with the girls throughout these past years, and one that they are not only still practicing, but are now teaching to their children and also teaching in classroom settings in their respective churches.

The understanding of the success of SETS came, these many years later, through words penned in letters and on thank-you cards received for wedding gifts and subsequent baby gifts. One young woman wrote, "I will definitely teach Cooper (her new baby) about SETS. Thank you for teaching me." Another wrote, "I still remember to look for SETS." And, as if to reassure me, another young woman wrote, "Don't worry, I still remember my SETS."

It is important to note at this point that the same girls were in my class every week for two years and that the SETS Method was taught to them every week they were in class. Teaching with consistency and reinforcement over time is critical to how well they retain what they have learned. For the concept to be long-lasting and life-changing, this process of thought must become second nature and something they do without even having to think about it. Then, and only then, will it become their anchor to God as they begin to recognize their gifts and release the spiritual music of their soul.

"Sow an act, reap a habit;
sow a habit, reap a character;
sow a character, reap a destiny."
G. D. Boardman

CHAPTER 3

SETS CHANGE LIVES

SETS provide hope for a bright tomorrow.

May I share with you the whisperings of the spirit, in the form of penned testimonials, as to the profound, long-lasting effect the practice of **S**piritually **E**nlightening **T**hought**s** (**SETS**) has had on the lives of the young women who were taught the SETS Method over eight years ago?

A MESSED-UP BATCH

As a teenager, one of my religious leaders taught me to look at life through spiritual eyes, eyes searching for direction and understanding of why I was here and where I was going. Though I cannot recall the first time I was introduced to the idea of **S**piritually **E**nlightening **T**hought**s** (SETS), I will forever remember reporting each Sunday on different spiritual experiences I had throughout the week. It was an opportunity that was fascinating and at the same time challenging. I believe that whether we are baking bread, applying make-up, or walking in the park we can find something in the process that will testify of a Father in Heaven, His Son Jesus Christ, and their plan for us.

For a teenager it requires a paradigm shift, perhaps, a shift from literal to spiritual eyes. Before, my thoughts were simple and in some ways self-centered, but when I was asked to find deeper meaning in life, to look beyond the obvious in nature and human processes, I was able to find spiritual meaning and connection in all things.

In our young women's group, each girl seemed to find layers of meaning for everyday activities and observations. By sharing personal insight on these experiences, I was able to find a relationship between somewhat abstract principles found in the scriptures and concrete manifestations in life of the same principles. I believe this is the reason SETS have such influence in a young girl's life. Youth desire so much to find out who they are and how they relate to the world around them. SETS have the ability to assure us that there is something beyond our worldly pursuits, there is something and someone greater in life, and all things testify to this spiritual end.

Several months ago, I was teaching some young women in church and I shared a SET with them. I had been making some bread that morning and the batch was not turning out; it was simply awful. Just as I was about to throw my dough in the garbage, my husband came in and said, "Let me take care of this. Let me try to do something with this dough." After my initial reluctance, I handed over the dough. To my surprise, he was able to make some delicious rolls.

Though this was a simple process, it had a meaningful effect on my spirituality. I told the young women that many times the world will tell us that we are a messed-up batch, that we should be thrown out; yet, there is One who can make out of us something we could never make on our own. I told them that they are never without hope, no matter what their peers may tell them. As I looked into the eyes of one of these girls, I saw tears welling and I knew that something in this experience had given her hope. SETS give hope.

If all things bear record of Him, then we too, have something of divinity in us. Through teaching youth to look for spiritual meaning in life, we can teach them to find spiritual meaning and purpose in themselves. <u>SETS continue to help me find spiritual depth in every aspect of my life. It is a process that, once started, becomes part of your normal routine, your thought process. You can't ponder on your encounters in life without recognizing a spiritual application.</u>

I find SETS especially helpful in parenthood. Now that I have a little boy of my own and another on the way, I have the great responsibility of teaching them to find God in their lives. As I ponder best how to teach my little three-year-old about his divine nature and spiritual purpose here on earth, I have come to believe that the best foundation is to begin with his spiritual beginnings.

I believe little children need to know that they are not of this earth, that they have a literal Father in Heaven who is perfect. By knowing their true heritage, children will be able to find spiritual qualities in everything they do.

The other day as I was hurrying Cooper out to the car to pick up daddy, he turned to me and said, "Look, there's a star. Did Heavenly Father make the stars?" I quickly said, "Yes, Cooper, he did." Then rushed to buckle him in his car seat. Still intent upon this answer, he questioned, "Did Heavenly Father make big brothers?" For a moment I paused and was taught by my little boy. Is this not the question that baffles philosophers throughout the ages: "Who am I?" At a young age, children are already questioning where they came from and sadly many at old age still wonder. After observing the beauty of the earth, Cooper began to question about the Creator. By teaching children about God, they will be able to give spiritual value to those things around them, the everyday experiences and observations. And this is a perfect foundation for teaching the idea of SETS. As Cooper gets older, his spiritual theories and parables may become more complex, but I pray he will always remember the simplicity of God's plan and be able to find examples of this plan in the shining sun, the blossoming fruit tree, or his mother's kiss.

Kathryn LeMone - (Cooper, and Isaiah's mommy who loves children's literature)

OH, GREAT, HOMEWORK FOR CHURCH

I remember the first time that you taught us about **S**piritually **E**nlightening **T**hought**s** (SETS) and you wanted us to find one during the week and tell you again on Sunday what we had come up with. My first thought was, "Oh, great, homework for church". I decided that I would do it anyway and <u>I don't think I've stopped since</u>. I have realized that God is everywhere and in everything. Of course, the entire earth is His creation, why wouldn't He be everywhere? SETS have helped me to recognize this.

From the smallest, most simple to the most grand and complicated of creations, He is there. We can find Him everywhere, because He loves us.

Emilee Shelton - (Massage Therapist)

A WARNING PAUSE

I reflect back on my first experiences with SETS and remember them to have greatly impacted my life, as they continue to do. They brought new meaning to everyday objects that I was surrounded by.

When first presented to me, I was unsure and doubtful as to whether I would be able to produce those spiritual thoughts myself. But as soon as I gave it a try, I realized how my thought process and constant spiritual-mindedness, on a daily basis, started to change. I began seeing so many things around me with an attitude of enrichment. A stop sign was not just a way of bringing a car to a halt, but it was a warning to me to bring my life to a halt and proceed with caution as I embarked on new journeys in my life; a warning to pause, evaluate my situation, my life, and consider every alternative of what might approach me ahead. This particular SET has gone through my mind several times when I've needed to make important, consequential decisions in my life. <u>I found that once I changed my thought process on a spiritual level, I couldn't stop!</u> I was constantly analyzing many items around me and discovering ways to relate them to my spiritual being. SETS gave me the opportunity to feel my spirit and the spirit of a higher being every day. I am grateful that I was exposed to such a wonderful way of seeing the world and relating my surroundings to my soul, my heart, and my mind.

Janel Duff - (2nd grade teacher who loves being outdoors)

HIGH SCHOOL VOLLEYBALL TEAM

As I begin to recollect my days as a young woman in our church, one of the first things I remember is being taught to have **S**piritually **E**nlightening **T**hought**s** (SETS). This was a special system of helping us to become more aware of our surroundings and their hidden spiritual meanings. We learned that we could find something spiritually enlightening in everything around us, if we just gave it a little thought.

When we were first introduced to SETS, I found myself being the one who couldn't seem to come up with an answer, but soon I got the hang of it. I began to find SETS in everything around me and in a lot of my life experiences. I can still remember the first SET that I shared with the class.

Another young woman in our class, Heather, and I were selling something door-to-door to raise money for our high school volleyball team. As we were continually turned away, we had a SET. As we walked, we talked about how difficult it must be to be a missionary and be rejected when trying to preach the gospel. We were a little embarrassed, but when Sunday came we shared our SET with the class and were quite pleased with ourselves. From that point on, finding SETS became easy. Here are some other specific examples I remember sharing with the class:

<u>A Compass</u>: A compass guides us and directs us to our destination. It can be likened unto the scriptures. We can use the scriptures to guide us in our daily lives and direct us to our destination, eternal life.

<u>A Tree</u>: Just as with a tree, our testimony can grow firm, tall, and strong, if we nurture it and feed it with scripture study, prayer, and living the gospel.

<u>A Chalkboard</u>: Because of the atonement, our sins can be forgiven and 'our slate can be wiped clean'.

Finding SETS became a fun and exciting challenge for all of us. We would try to find SETS in every object and in every experience we encountered. I personally found myself to be much more aware of the things around me, and I recognized God's love for me. Finding something spiritual in everything around you helps you to stay in tune with your Heavenly Father and better able to listen to the promptings of the Holy Ghost.

I am now married with two children, and I am teaching the young women in my church. <u>I have introduced SETS to my class and enjoy watching them grow each week as they become more in tune with God. I am also excited to teach my children to find SETS in all of their surroundings, as it will help them to recognize their divine nature and the tremendous love God has for them.</u>

Jennie Slade – (a wife to her best friend Chad, mother of Taylor and Jackson and lover of Latin music)

'ON HOLD' UNTIL I MATURED

When you first asked me to share my thoughts about SETS for this book, I spent some time just putting myself back into the classroom and the context in which I was introduced to SETS. In our class, I always felt I was in a safe environment and knew I was accepted - just as I was! There was no expectation to be anything more than what I was, and all lessons were taught in a framework that was accessible and applicable to my experience at that time. This concept is also central to what I interpreted to be the essence of what SETS are.

So often in religious settings, as a youth, I felt like spirituality was something to be achieved when I was older, when I was better, or when I was more worthy. I felt like my experiences were somehow inadequate, and I was sort of 'on hold' until I matured. When I was introduced to SETS, I came away with such a different feeling; suddenly my spirituality wasn't dependent on my being older, wiser, or better. I only had to be willing to be present and aware now, in the moment, and spiritual experiences will arise out of that. Spirituality was suddenly all around me, and I simply had to choose to be a part of it. This is empowering for a 15-year-old who is always striving to be something else and fulfill someone else's expectations. During adolescence we spend so much time focusing on what we aren't, but practicing SETS allowed me to have a greater sense of integrity and deeper connection with what is good in the world and within me. My life experiences became less insignificant, and I more readily accepted that where I was spiritually was where I was supposed to be.

As an adult these concepts have become even more relevant, particularly since I've become a mother. So much of parenting is filled with mundane routines of caring for the temporal needs of children, and it's so easy to get the sense that each day is filled with nothing! <u>When SETS are a part of every day and every moment, I realize that my days filled with feeding, clothing and bathing a child are all spiritual practices; I simply have to choose to make them such.</u>

SETS have given me a nonjudgmental context to examine my life; it's not about what's good or bad, it's about learning from my choices and being open to what God or the universe has to offer me.

Amanda Suarez – (full time student, full time mother, and part time massage therapist)

PART II

THE AWAKENING

"Our birth is but a sleep and a forgetting:
The soul that rises with us, our life's star,
Hath had elsewhere its setting,
And cometh from afar:
Not in entire forgetfulness,
And not in utter nakedness,
But trailing clouds of glory do we come
From God, who is our home:
Heaven lies about us in our infancy!"
- William Wordsworth

"If a child is to keep alive his inborn sense of wonder without any such gift from the fairies, he needs the companionship of at least one adult who can share it, rediscovering with him the joy, excitement and mystery of the world we live in."
Rachel Carson

CHAPTER 4

WELCOME TO A CHILD'S WORLD

Before we begin to teach children, it is important to have an
understanding of and be able to view the world through their eyes.

When was the last time you walked outside late at night and gazed at the majesty of the night sky with its myriad of stars seeming to twinkle to the beat of some unheard symphony, or went barefoot in the grass? How long has it been since you took a walk in the woods, stopped next to a tall, majestic pine tree, pulled a pine branch close to you, and tried to see how many pinecones you could count? When did you last walk on the beach and feel the sand sift between your toes, or pick a budding rose and then, one by one, pull the petals off in search of some magical treasure that lay hidden in the center?

Welcome to a child's world where everything is new and yet to be learned. Where curiosity and exploring have not yet been replaced by the rush and misguided urgency of our adult, everyday life. It has been said that the sadness in life comes not from what we experience but from the realization of what we have missed.

Welcome to the child's world where simple pleasures bring joy and wonder. As we observe a child, curious, exploring, and wanting to understand this mortal life they have been born into, we see how open and receptive they are to their surroundings. They seem to be saying, "Here I am. I'm new here. I want to feel all there is to feel, see all there is to see, and do all there is to do. I want to explore and experience life. I want to feel safe, loved, and accepted. I want to hug my dog and have him kiss me back. I want to look at the night sky and wonder why the stars twinkle and how it all began. I want to build sand castles, then wonder when the churning surf crept in and swirled my castle into the sea, fragmenting it once again into tiny particles of sand lying in wait for the next child with a new dream. I want to feel the breeze as it blows against my skin and in the springtime try to catch raindrops in my mouth. I want to run, dance, and twirl around, but most of all, I want to feel safe, accepted, and loved unconditionally."

When my children were little, Andrea about 6 and Troy about 4 years old, I took them to something that was called a 'Petting Zoo'. This 'zoo,' as it was loosely named, traveled from town to town, and in each found its home in the parking lot of a supermarket or anyplace with the potential for a massive amount of customers during the day. The animal menagerie was composed of a varied assortment of farm animals ranging from pot-bellied pigs to Nubian goats. All friendly, knowing that their constant supply of food was just a click of the vending machine away and that they would be fed by the eager hand of a waiting child. Of course, the feeding part of the interaction between child and animal directly lead to the 'petting' part. Hence the name 'Petting Zoo.'

Andrea and Troy were overjoyed at petting the rabbits, baby goats, and trying to pet the chickens and ducks. Have you ever tried petting a chicken? 'About face and run after you get fed,' seems to be their motto and all that is on their mind. Oops, I said mind. Now, when we are talking about chickens, that's up for debate.

Everything went well until all of a sudden Andrea began to scream. She needed comforting. Why on earth is she crying? Look at all of these cute, sweet, lovable animals around her. Oh, I see, her shoe's untied. Maybe she stepped on her shoelace and almost tripped. I'd better take care of that. I crouched down, sitting nearly on my heels, and began to tie her shoe, when one of the biggest goats I have ever seen in my life nuzzled up behind me and began to chew on my hair. Actually, it got worse. In what seemed like a split second, the goat must have decided that the sweater I had on reminded him of something he had eaten before that was very succulent, and before I knew it, he had a mouthful of my sweater with a little of me thrown in for good measure. No wonder Andrea was terrified. From her short vantage point, the goat to her looked like a huge monster with only one thing on its mind (goats do have a mind, of sorts), nuzzling close enough to the human body to see what's on today's menu of succulent nibbles.

Once I placed myself in the child's world, I could then see and understand life from their perspective. And again I say, welcome to a child's world.

Why, when a child is open to understanding and learning, do we as one all-knowing seem to say, "Hurry and grow up so you can get on with life and center all of your focus on learning life skills so you can get a good job, live in a big house, and then you will be of worth." We seem to say, "Focus on the things of the world and through them you will find success and joy." This is the thinking of modern society and the aim of academia. Everywhere a child turns, he or she is taught to conform, color within the lines, don't dawdle, just hurry, don't sing, be quiet. Have you ever wondered how many Michelangelos, Tolstoys, and Shakespeares there are wandering around in this world with gifts and talents that are lying dormant in the garden of their lives, not having received the proper nutrients to enable them to develop the potential that lies within? Have they been halted in their endeavor to learn who they are and how they relate to this world? Have they been told to conform to a 'norm' and to forget about the creative side of themselves? After all, this is the 21st - century and we measure our success by what we have and, you child, are going to do that too. We ask them to conform to a model that is broken, a world that is confused, and then wonder why there is excessive overuse of drugs and alcohol. We seemingly have forgotten the most important task that a child can learn to do - learn to connect with God. Our society does not teach it. We generally do not even give it the 'time of day.' We are too busy doing the things that increase visual stature and glory. We are too 'fixed on the things of the world.'

It has been erroneously assumed by some, that it is enough to impart good teachings on an infrequent basis. That somehow notes will be added to the page of music already written in the child's mind, but what about the heavenly music yet unsung? Music yet unwritten, lying dormant in the child's soul – waiting for a spark, a connection to activate it. The flower needs water and nutrients to grow, and we need to be fed and nurtured by the spirit to be able to sing the songs that lie deep within us all.

Teenagers. As we look at childhood, it is important that we spend a portion of this time talking about teenagers.

Teenagers have special trials to deal with as they try to define who they are and how to relate to the world around them. Some of that discovery comes from within, but the majority comes from their peer group and what they perceive others think of them. The teenage years are very precarious times for youth if they have not received the needed love and support in their homes, and if they have looked to others to provide their definitions. It is a confusing time fraught with many opportunities to make decisions that will have far-reaching, lifelong consequences. Some of those consequences can continue into generations to come and are hard to 'make right.'

The teenage years are full of temptations and choices that are made, many times, without parental guidance. If the parents are not there, the choices are made at school or after school, and are not made within the walls of the home. These are choices of honesty, modesty, virtue, and the list goes on. How the teenager approaches these choices and eventually resolves the choice with an action depends in a great part on what voice they are listening to. Is it their peers? The anger they hold inside or their inner voice and what is that voice telling them? Is it feelings of worthlessness? Do they feel as though they are in a situation that is hopeless? Do they feel trapped in actions that take them deeper and deeper into sorrow such as drug or alcohol abuse?

Or is the teenager lucky, with a loving support group, and a family that provides continual rein-forcement by showing love and acceptance, gently guiding them to all that is good and wholesome. When the teenager listens to their inner voice, is it reassuring? Does it confirm that they are of worth and that they have a Heavenly Father who loves them? Does that inner voice tell them to connect with God when they have a problem, and that by doing so they can receive the guidance needed for their life and lead them to find joy? Do they realize that they are an important part of the larger plan of God and that these small, hurtful, confusing moments are just a blink in the eye of time? Do they understand that they, in partnership with God, can accomplish great miracles? Do they understand that by recognizing the connection to God in all things and having **S**piritually **E**nlightening **T**hought**s** (SETS), they can change their life for the better as their footsteps continually walk toward the light?

Children who are ill. As we continue to look at a child's world it is important for us to note that there are many children who are in situations that they find almost terrifying, and one of those situations is illness.

Children who are seriously ill need a great deal of reassurance, comfort, and love. They need to understand that they are children of God and that He loves them unconditionally and will always be with them, bringing comfort during times of uncertainty and fear. It is about one such child that I wish to speak.

SOMEONE TO WATCH OVER ME

Let me tell you a story. It goes something like this: Once upon a time there was a four-year-old girl with long blonde hair and hazel eyes who lived on the east coast in a beautiful little cottage and who was very seriously ill. Her parents were told by the doctor that they must move to find a dry climate that would agree with the little girl or she might not survive another winter. So, the mother and father sold everything, bought a travel trailer, left their home and families, and set out in search of warmer weather, for they did not want to lose their only child.

First, they went to Florida. It was beautiful there, but the climate was too damp and the little girl was very sick. They moved to Texas, but that didn't work either. California was their next stop, and they settled in a small town called Banning. The little girl seemed better for a while but still had some dangerous bouts with her illness. After a couple of years the little girl began to get very weak, so her parents accepted the advice of a friend and took her to an acclaimed specialist in childhood diseases.

Sometimes she would get scared when she heard mommy and the doctors talking because it didn't sound good to her little girl's understanding. She didn't want to die, even though she didn't understand exactly what dying meant. But it sounded like something she didn't want to do since she would have to leave her mommy, daddy, and her dog Lizzy. So, she talked to God a lot and He spoke back. It was almost as if she could feel Him hold her when her fever got really high.

Her doctor seemed like a nice man. She had gotten used to his kindness and wasn't too frightened, until he suggested to her mother that they see another doctor, a radiologist. You see, they found tumors that were very close to the brain. That's when the doctors decided that they were too close to the brain to operate so the decision was made to try a relatively new procedure. That's when she got really scared. She prayed to her Heavenly Father that He would go with her and never leave her.

When they got to the doctor's office where the first treatment would be given, they were ushered into a large room with a table that was supposed to be a bed, but the little girl knew it was really a table with a thin mattress on top. The kind doctors and nurses helped her onto the table and explained that they were going to put 'war paint,' in non-removable pen, on her face in three places. One 'x' on each temple and one 'x' in the middle of her forehead down between her eyes. The doctors told her that the treatments wouldn't hurt but that she would have to lie very still, not move a muscle, and breath very softly. They told her that she would hear a loud clicking sound coming from the big machine, but nothing would even touch her. The procedure was to use radiation to destroy the tumors. They were hoping this would save the child's life.

The treatments, each aiming an unseen beam at one of the 'x's, were administered three times a week for twelve weeks for a total of 36 treatments. Every time the little girl got on the table she knew she had to lie ever so still or bad things would happen. She would pray to God and ask Him to stay with her because she was so very frightened. And He stayed. You see, while these treatments were being administered everyone had to leave the room, and the little girl was left alone in the big cold room with the bright lights and the big machine that made the loud clicking sounds. And God was there too, giving her courage and whispering love to her spirit. It wasn't so bad with God there.

When the treatments first began, she was not too dizzy when she got off the table, but as they progressed, with every treatment she became dizzier and it was harder to walk. By the end of the cycle of treatments she was a little sick but God told her she would be okay. And she believed Him. The doctors said they had given her so much radiation to kill the tumors, that if this series of treatments didn't work, she could not have any more because she had been given the maximum radiation dosage. No more radiation until it all dissipated from her little body and that would be years. So, the family hoped and prayed and the little girl talked to God, and He told her how much He loved her and that everything would be all right. And it was.

Oh, to have the faith of a child for they are so loved by God. They are a joy unto Him and He is their comforter.

How many children are there that are sick and in need of comfort? To be able to give the gift of understanding of how to connect with God to a child that is sick, in need of comfort, and frightened of things they don't understand, would be a blessing indeed. To be able to give that gift to a child who is not feeling well and perhaps doesn't even know what feeling well really means. To offer up a little spark of divinity and to wipe away all their tears. To be able to reach out and provide a glimpse of heaven and help them to understand the great love God has for them would be the greatest gift one could give.

"Let your light so shine before men,
that they may see your good works,
and glorify your Father which is in heaven."
St. Matthew 5:16

CHAPTER 5

GIFTS OF THE SPIRIT

A gift, as the word implies, is given by the gift giver to the gift recipient.
And if life is the party, everyone comes with a gift. No one comes empty-handed.

We all enter this world with special, unique qualities and gifts. They are ours alone to have and to develop in our own way, the way God intended. These gifts may be unlike anyone else's, since each is given specific to the individual. Gifts are to be nurtured and developed with the love and understanding that these are the things that make us magnificently unique. These are the gifts that shout to be heard and long to be fulfilled. When God has granted a gift, that gift is ever present, trying to find expression. Just as a painter needs a canvas and a singer needs a song, so all gifts need their appointed manner of expression.

Nurturing of gifts by parents, teachers, or caregivers who are in tune with the spirit is part of the healthy development process for the child. Only after they recognize that each child has unique gifts and can respect that individual uniqueness can they nurture and prepare the child to develop the gift to its fullest form. First, they must acknowledge the child's potential, then they must understand their role in nurturing the child so that the gift will be allowed to blossom to maturity.

As the following parable of *The Potter And The Lump Of Clay* illustrates, we each need a divinely led guide to show the way and help awaken the slumbering gift, releasing its beauty to the world.

THE POTTER AND THE LUMP OF CLAY

Once upon a time in the land of far away there lived a noble knight. Oh, his name could have been Lancelot or Gareth; but it was Thomas who lived in a world where gold coin and power ruled. How noble it is that a man would do good without being asked. To serve with no reward for service other than to make an honest wage, for he was a potter of men. He molded the spirits into good vessels to carry the living water to all the world.

The potter set out of town one day to find a bit of clay that would be perfect to mold into an object of great beauty. As the potter walked the path, he heard the clay along the way shouting, "Choose me. Choose me, for I will bend to your every touch and mold myself to your every wish." And the potter replied, "It is not you that I desire, for I need clay with inborn fiber to allow me just to guide, for it is a union between the clay and the master that produces the greatest treasures. For if you are molded with no thought of the innate ability that lies within, there is only half as good a piece to make for it is only half the goodness turned within. For both must express themselves at their best, the potter and the lump of clay."

And the potter chose another clay, one with inborn fiber. And they worked together all the day until the night held soft the moon and the potter stopped the wheel. Should he stop too soon before the clay was formed, a half-completed piece would be. So he began again and together they worked through the unending night, the potter and the lump of clay.

As the potter sat in the barn and dreamed a dream of creating, he asked God to bless him with knowledge. As his wheel moved and his hands guided the wooden potter's knife to and fro across the clay, the image of a vessel began to form. If he had a hardness of heart and pressed too hard against the wooden knife, the object he was tenderly trying to sculpt would become distorted and lose the shape it was intended to be. Ever so tenderly, he would press the knife against the clay as his foot pressed the pedal back and forth and the wheel began to spin.

The pressure had to be there, but not too much. The wheel had to be made to spin, but not too fast. In the potter's strong hands and keen eye was love for the object that was but a dream to be created; forming gently, nudging the clay into the shape of its potential. Gently he would mold. On occasion he would press too hard then draw back in anguish, not meaning to destroy the image of the potter's hand.

Day after day and with relentless love, the potter turned the wheel. All the time praying that the clay would find its' form and bend in harmony with the pressure; so the clay, with its innate beauty and form, and the potter, with his wisdom and knowledge, could together create a work to carry the gift of love.

In harmony they worked through the endless night until at last was formed, by the potter's wheel and the lump of clay, a new vessel of great beauty. And all came from far and wide to view the treasure there, for the lump of clay and the potter fair had released the beauty in them both as they worked together creating, the master's hand - the willing clay. Each giving their all. Each doing their part. The potter and the lump of clay.

Gifts, always looking for expression, need a 'Potter,' a guide, to provide the needed direction for their development.

What happens if the child doesn't have nurturing parents or if the child has not had an opportunity, in a family setting, to express the gift? Just because there is no guidance of interested parents to help nurture the gift does not mean that the expression of the gift will not manifest itself in a positive manner. For it certainly may if the owner of the gift seeks God's guidance in recognizing and developing it. However, many times it is very difficult for the child to outwardly recognize the gift as there may be feelings of humility involved and they may not recognize the gift in themselves.

If we accept the fact that thoughts are the precursors to actions, then we must also recognize that if thoughts are not positive, the avenue of expression may be inappropriate and lean toward the base rather than the righteous. If we are to acknowledge that each one of us has unique gifts, then we must also understand and believe that the genre of expression will be based on prior thought.

If a person has the gift of writing and the thoughts are less than pure, and the one owning the gift has allowed themselves to be overtaken by negative thoughts, then the gift of writing may respond by writing some seamy, steamy tale. The same would be true of the gift of music, drawing, or oil painting.

If the thoughts are base, then the drawings or paintings may be base and less than desirable. Even though the owner of the gift has found a manner of expression, since it is not expressed in a manner that God has intended, the individual may continue searching for fulfillment, not realizing that fulfillment will only come when the gift is developed in God's way.

Could the gift, while unfulfilled and in need of expression, manifest itself in negative behavior if there is no other avenue for the expression to be released? Could this cause confusing, pent-up anxiety that may not be understood? For example, Johnny really likes to dance and at a very young age his dancing is cute and even encouraged by the parents. As Johnny grows up, however, his parents begin to suggest other points of focus to try to dissuade Johnny from dancing because, as he gets older, they feel dancing is a less desirable thing to do. Then the parents, in their infinite wisdom, give him fencing and karate lessons. Of course, Johnny wants to please his parents, so he acquiesces to their desires when all the time the little voice, longing for expression, wants to dance.

Failing to nurture and develop our gifts can lead to an acute sense that there is a part of us left unfulfilled. It is as though 80% of us developed and matured, leaving the 20% that was the gift left wanting.

**"A musician must make music, an artist must paint, a poet must write,
if he is to be at peace with himself. What a man can be, he must be."
Abraham Maslow**

Youth is the time to recognize the talent or gift and nurture it into full bloom then see where it leads. It would be almost impossible to play catch-up later in life unless the talent has been nurtured along the way. Nothing can substitute for the years of development of the gift. The gift may still develop at an age older than youth, but it may not develop as completely had the enthusiastic development begun as a child. As we look at playing the piano for instance, which requires manual dexterity. If a child learns when young, the physical ability develops in the hands as the child grows, and the hands are strengthened for reach and proper movement across the keys. A person many years beyond childhood cannot expect the flexibility of the child. It's not there. It is important to note, however, that on occasion, but ever so rarely, a 'miracle' occurs whereby the unrecognized, un-nurtured gift manifests itself later in life. The owner of the gift seems to possess some 'magical powers,' as if to have had the gift almost subconsciously taught, and the now-recognized gift manifests itself in a nearly developed form. However, this is extremely rare.

Now having said this, it must be emphasized: **No matter what our age, it is essential we understand that we each have God given gifts that are lying dormant, waiting for their awakening. And at the time when desire meets action, the beauty of the gift acknowledged and released will bring fulfillment and joy in the life of its owner and bless the lives of all with whom it has been shared.**

The time is now for us to ASK God to help us find our gift, then to SEEK after the development of our gift, KNOCK and the way shall be opened, and we will find the joy and fulfillment that comes from following God's plan and, thus, striving to reach the full measure of the potential that lies within each of us. But we must connect with God first and enlist His aid and guidance. It is never too late.

Children in innocence are many times unaware of the gifts they possess - gifts ever searching for voice. That is why it is essential for them to have an early close connection with God so that He can lead the way. If children can understand early on that they have unique gifts, they can then be taught to go to God for answers to the question of how to express and fulfill their gift. As their communication with God strengthens, grows deeper, and the trust level increases, they will be more open to the guidance and inspiration given. They will go to God with their questions – listening for the answers. When the child is the seeker, the answers and direction will come from one who loves unconditionally, and that someone is God.

So, as we talk about the great potential of children and the development of their gifts, we understand that they must have a connection to God in order to stay on the path and be able to unlock their full potential.

Through practicing the SETS Method, the heart is awakened to the music of the soul. Once this happens, the gifts are brought to focus as the child receives guidance from God, enabling them to seek out the gift and understand the steps needed to develop it. God is the giver of the gift, the nurturer of the soul, and as the giver He chose the gift. He picked it out, wrapped it, tied the ribbon, and delivered the gift to the child with a gift tag that reads, "Ask! Seek! Knock!" But children can't ask if they are confused about whom to ask. They can't seek if they won't recognize God when they see Him. And they can't knock if they can't find the door. By connecting with God, children will be able to do all three. By maintaining a closeness to God and recognizing Him when He speaks, how great their joy will be; how great a fulfillment they will feel; how much love they will be able to give as they share their gift with others; and how much love this connection will bring to a child by giving them feelings of worth and acceptance.

POTENTIAL

"In the breast of the bulb is the promise of spring.

In the little blue egg is the bird that will sing.

In the sole of the seed is the hope of the sod.

In the heart of the child is the Kingdom of God."

W. L. Sidger

CHAPTER 6

AWAKENING THE POTENTIAL OF A CHILD

It is vital that the child is viewed as one with great future potential.

It is important that we understand that children are not devoid of talent. We do not live in a barren desert without nourishment for the soul. Divinity is all around us. We must but pause for a moment, become aware, see, really see, maybe for the first time, all that God has placed here for us. Then will we be able to recognize the bud of talent and true gifts that lie within each child. These gifts were meant to be developed to not only edify the child and help them find joy, but to edify the world around them. And as the gift is developed, they will become like a candle in the dark night lighting the way. When coming upon one whose candle has not yet been lit or whose flame has gone out, they will be able to give the needed light until the other can steady their candle, turn away from the chill wind, and, once again, rekindle their own light. And as they light the way for another, their candle will seem to burn brighter and take on a deeper glow.

As parents, teachers, and caregivers of children, we need to turn our hearts and thoughts to the child and ponder what we can do to assist them as they find their way along the unlit path, and to do this we need to be in partnership with God. We need to evaluate whether our light is bright enough for others to follow and ask ourselves the following questions: Would we want the child to follow us along the path we currently tread? Can we lead the way? Do we know the way? Who or what is leading us? Is it righteousness and God's will or are we led by another voice calling to us across the valley of despair? We must define the journey. Before we can <u>show</u> the way we must <u>know the way</u> and identify the path of our own journey. Where do we want it to lead? Each step directs us to the destination. Is our destination one to which we would want to lead a child? On the journey to our destination, will the child be able to develop to their full potential?

As children, they left their Father's side to come to earth to fulfill their great potential. Then, sometimes through no fault of their own, earthly circumstances begin to snuff out their light, little by little, until its glow can hardly be seen in the slumber of night. If the child has lost its way and fallen prey to the ills of the world, it does not mean that all is lost. To the contrary, it merely means that the child, who longs for the light, needs someone, a guide with a strong bright light of their own, to lead them safely back to the path. Let me illustrate this point with the parable entitled *Rikka*.

RIKKA

My friend Tom has a magnificent Great Dane named Rikka. They go hiking every morning in the mountains behind his home, where Rikka is allowed to run free to explore and perhaps, if she is lucky, find the trail of a rabbit. A few weeks ago on their morning hike Rikka was lured farther and farther away from the path by the cunning voice of a coyote who, thinking that if he got her away from the protection of her master, he could then attack. The coyote had to lure her far enough away so that she could not hear her master's calls. As she got farther away, her master's voice became faint in the distance. She was innocent, and the call of adventure was so strong that she did not understand the dangers that lay ahead.

Tom spent much time calling and searching, afraid of what the outcome would be if he didn't find Rikka quickly. He then asked God to help him find her. Within minutes, as he reached the crest of a hill, he saw Rikka and knew that his prayer had been answered.

Our children are many times very much like Rikka, leaving the trail in response to a cunning yet unfamiliar voice. Leaving the safety of the Master to follow some vague desire, totally unaware of the dangers that lie ahead.

As children grow up in today's world, we see them, with a great deal of confusion, trying to make sense out of it all. The negative voices are so strong that the counterbalance voices of good are many times overlooked not only by the child but also by the parents as well, as they rush to fulfill some ill conceived, misguided goal. We live in a world full of myriads of voices all shouting for our attention. It is a 21st - century filled with the static of life that seems to blast interference into our world as to suffocate the still small voice of the Master. This 21st - century voice tells us that this life is all about money, power, sex, fame, compromising values, and being right.

Children need to be able to separate from the world, be aware, and listen for the voice that will lead them safely home. They need an anchor to hold onto in the storms of life and someone, without a cunning hidden agenda, who will lead them upon the righteous path. Someone who is safe, that they know they can trust, who will accept them and love them unconditionally, and that someone is God. Our children need to be able to connect with God so that they, like Rikka, can hear the Master's voice when He calls to lead them safely home.

They need someone to help them trust again and to help them understand and be aware of

God's unconditional love for them. They may be lost and frightened and all they need to be shown is that they are not alone, that He is always there for them, and that all they have to do is ASK, SEEK, KNOCK, and it shall be opened for them. It is difficult for children to do this without the loving guidance of parents and extended family support. They may thrash around, wrenching to and fro because they are young, vulnerable, and in need of guidance and direction, and many times have been so confused by the world that they don't know where to go to find it. Sometimes those that were sent to protect them caused great damage and harm, and trust and innocence were lost for a time. However, all is not lost. As long as there is a belief and connection to God, there is always hope for a bright future. But there must be someone who gently leads them back to the path, and to lead the way you must know the destination. So it's up to each one of us to recognize His hand in all things, practice seeing with our spiritual eyes, and evaluate where we are in our own journey. We need to reconnect ourselves to God and reach out to the child on this ever-winding path as we guide them to receive the fullness of joy that God has reserved for each of His children.

And as we again ask, "Where are the Beethovens, Bachs, and Picassos?" We are answered, "They are among us, yet to be discovered, and with the right nourishment and encouragement, they will blossom." All we have to do is awaken the gifts and talents that already exist in the child and in us. We need to ride the wind of discovery and embrace who we can become. We need to throw aside fear and step forward and reach deep into our souls and ask God to guide us as we begin to look at life with our spiritual eyes. And as we begin to see more clearly through the lens of the spirit, we will recognize the signs God has placed along the way to guide us and direct our path. We just need to **"Ask, and it shall be given you; seek, and ye shall find; knock, and it shall be opened unto you." (St. Matthew 7:7)**

When a child is born, their world is new and one to be experienced. As they begin their mortal journey, children are like magnets, drawing to themselves both the positive and the negative, the good and the bad that cross their paths. To be a child is to be one who will receive teachings and be taught. This experience can either be positive or negative, depending upon what is served up to a child in their buffet of life experiences. It is the truly fortunate child who has parents and extended family members to nurture and love them; parents who strive to recognize the gifts within the child and use every means to help them develop and reach their full potential. This is not an easy task for the parents, for it means that they must give to another and forget self.

Severely handicapped children. Reaching out to children who are severely handicapped is perhaps one of the most challenging, heart-wrenching, heart-warming, selfless, and fulfilling things a parent or caregiver can do. Many times it takes all of the energy, patience, and resolve one can muster. It is a situation where every small step takes monumental effort and where each small achievement is welcomed with open arms and enthusiasm. It is a circumstance where finding, understanding, and then aiding the handicapped child in the search and fulfillment of their potential seems like a daunting task. But each of God's children does have potential, however distant that potential may seem. It is important that we do not give up but recognize that even the severely handicapped child has a God-given measure of potential to be fulfilled.

Helen Keller, who could neither see nor hear, in her book so aptly entitled *Optimism*, explains, "I long to accomplish a great and noble task; but it is my chief duty and joy to accomplish humble tasks as though they were great and noble." She dedicated this book to her teacher.

The affect of true love by a family for a child. Giving the gift of love to a child stricken with an illness so severe as to not allow the child to respond with mutual love is emulating the true, unconditional love of God. It is about one such family that I wish to speak. Their names are Scott, the father; Laurie, the mother; and Nathan, David, Danielle, Rebecca, and Michael, the children. They are the Swain family.

David, who is now seventeen years old, suffered a series of strokes before birth that left him with cerebral palsy as well as severe mental retardation. Yet this young family has kept him at home, included him in all of the family gatherings, photos, and events, and tried, with every fiber of their being, to help him reach his full potential, however limited that may be. Because of this, David has developed far beyond the early predictions of his doctors and caregivers. No, he does not speak nor can he care for himself, but he has been exposed to the caring and nurturing of a loving family that provided the environment for his continued development and growth.

It is also important to note at this time that caring for David has not been at the expense of the other children in the family. They have each been lead by wise, loving parents to develop their own individual talents. They excel in music and dance and have proficiency beyond their years. These developed talents reflect even greater significance when we consider the unselfish service and care each has given to David over the years. He has truly been a blessing in their lives.

The following parable in letter form, called *David's Song*, was penned with this in mind. It embraces those things perhaps he would tell his family - if only he could speak.

DAVID'S SONG

Here am I, but a boy and what do you know of me? The road I tread has been strewn with unimaginable obstacles, painful both physically and mentally, for my body feels the pain of my afflictions. I cry to the Father in the night, for the anguish of my earthly prison is sometimes more than I can bear. The road has been long and hard and I am so very tired and desire to be with my Father once again, but my earthly mission is not yet fulfilled.

Because of my affliction, I have been allowed the memory of my Heavenly home and the sure knowledge of God. This has been a great comfort to me. Oh, how I wish I could tell you even the smallest part of what I know and have seen. Father bade that I can tell you no more than this, that I was one of the valiant spirits back in time before the world was. He told me of His great love for me and has taught me of the eternities that I might reach the full measure of my understanding.

Who am I, you ask? I am one who has been sent by the Father. I am he who, in the time before the earth was formed, said, "I will go, send me." I am he who sang with the choirs of angels and wrote songs for the Heavens to sing, for music is my life and my joy. Why did I come to earth in this manner, you ask? Did I not know this earth life would be filled with suffering and torment? Did I not know how difficult the task would be and how long the road home? How then could I make a choice such as this?

Long ago, before we were an earthly family, I was walking in a beautiful forest of tall trees and colorful flowers where all nature was in harmony. It was nearing time for me to make my decision. I knew that my intellect was keen and my body strong and erect. Could I go down and take upon myself a different form? Did I love enough? Could I complete the heavy task that was laid out before me? Was I strong enough to accept what lies ahead? I have never thought of myself as one with boundless courage. When Father and I spoke, I was so very willing to fulfill the plan, but I then became frightened. As I was trying to compose my thoughts I heard God's voice speak out to me. He said that oft times before we can fully express the songs of the heart, we must develop a depth of feeling that comes only from sacrifice, unconditional love, and service. I knew that for me to have the capacity to develop that depth of expression, I would have to experience earth life in a manner of sacrifice and love, as you would have to experience it in a manner of compassion and selfless service. How you ask, could I make such a choice? My dear family, there was no choice to make. I came because I love you.

You see, my coming in this manner gave you the opportunity to reach into the deepest part of your souls and discover the beauty, gifts, and talents that abound within. As you sought to assist with my daily needs, your depth of character grew, enabling you to give rise to the great gifts that you possess. As I watch you grow and the talents within you burn, I more fully understand my role in this great plan. My sacrifice in coming to earth so afflicted, your sacrifice of service, compassion, and love, each interdependent upon the other.

And again if you ask of me, "Why did you come?"

I shall answer, "I came because I love you."

I know it hasn't been easy for you. Loving and serving unconditionally is sometimes very difficult. From you I have learned what it means to sacrifice in love. To look beyond the outward appearance to the greater spirit that dwells within. Because of this earthly experience I have grown in patience, humility, and more fully understand the receiving of love, for each gift of your love expressed provides me such welcome relief and joy. These are rich blessings in my life and will be in the worlds to come. How I long to be able to speak to you and tell you of my great love for you. The love, kindness, and compassion you have shown to me over these years has touched my soul and been an anthem to my spirit.

> Thank you for giving me time in your life and caring for one so afflicted.
>
> Thank you for assisting me to grow and develop.
>
> Thank you for your faith, always knowing that the mortal shell you see before
>
> you is but an earthly cloak I wear.
>
> Thank you for believing that who I am is greater than who you see.
>
> Thank you for loving me.

I shall be eternally grateful for all you have done for me. For your nurturing, love, and compassion. Please know that this earth life and our intertwined existence is part of a magnificent plan of a Father who loves us. And when my song has been sung, I shall go and prepare a place of joy where we can sing together with the choirs of angels and bask in the light of His love.

This earthly life is my path to a glorious eternity. Thank you for being part of my journey.

Know that I love you.

Your son,

David

All children are not as fortunate as David who is loved unconditionally, not only by God but his family as well.

For children, when proper nurturing is not available as they are growing up, the strong, negative influences that they may be faced with seem to strangle all hope of reaching their potential by the development of their God-given gifts. Then the children, not having had proper guidance and having had less than desirable experiences, may not even know that they are children of God and that He loves them unconditionally. They may not understand that there are gifts within them awaiting expression. It may not even enter their minds. Not even a remote possibility. It may only be when the child can control their own safe environment that the gifts begin to manifest themselves. So it may be many years before a vision of their potential is offered in a quiet moment of connection with God. However, if they can connect with God early in their development, then the understanding of the gift will be made known at a younger age.

He does not give a gift and not provide a way to develop it. Everyone has a song that needs to be sung, and the guidance will be provided to enable us to sing it and fulfill the potential that lies within each one of us.

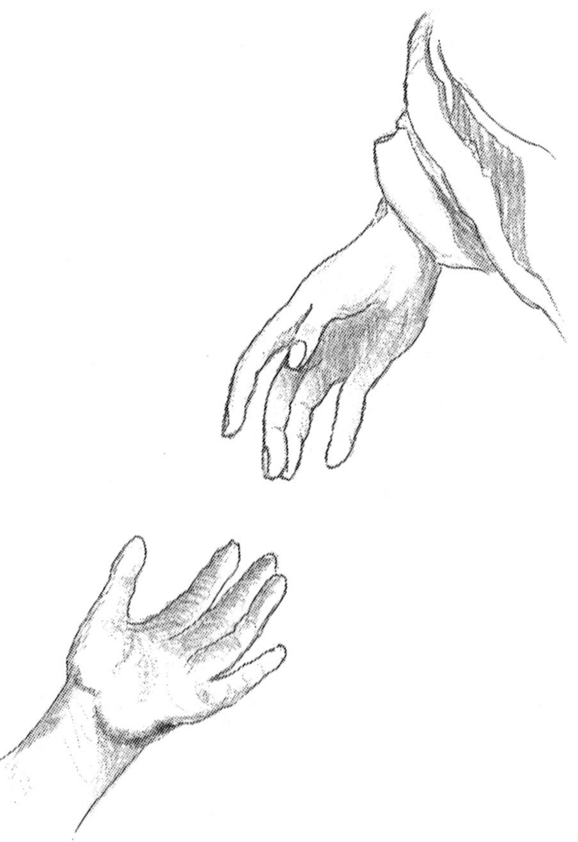

PART III

BEGIN WITH YOURSELF

"What we are is God's gift to us.
What we become is our gift to God."
Author Unknown

"Happiness isn't something that depends on our surroundings, Corrie.

It's something we make inside ourselves."

The Hiding Place

Corrie ten Boom

CHAPTER 7

BEGIN WITH YOURSELF

One person can make a difference,
but first you must begin with yourself.

Imagine with me for a moment that you are a high school junior attending ABC High School. Your English Literature teacher was just about to begin teaching an in-depth study of Shakespeare's *King Henry VIII*. Over the past week he had prepared your class by familiarizing you with Shakespeare's life story and style of writing so that you would have the background to better understand the words he penned.

The day the teacher was to begin *King Henry VIII*, he became seriously ill and a substitute teacher was suddenly called in. The substitute was, of all things, the boy's Physical Education teacher and coach of the high school football team. Now, I don't know what that image conjures up in your mind but in mine it yells out, "Won't be learning about Shakespeare!" The P.E. teacher knows football and, although some may think that football and Shakespeare are in the same league, I have serious doubts about that. Have you ever heard a football player quote *King Henry VIII* as they made the final touchdown? *"I have touch'd the highest point of all my greatness, And from that full meridian of my glory I haste now to my setting."* I don't think so. That substitute teacher doesn't have the knowledge, and more importantly, the passion for Shakespeare to be able to teach the subject effectively to the class. His passion is football. If it was English Literature, he would be teaching it. You can't teach what you do not know.

Begin with yourself. Before you begin *Teaching Children How To Connect With God,* it is essential that you learn the principles you will be teaching. You need passion for the subject matter and the power of your convictions that you have experienced positive changes in your own life. You must have belief in the effectiveness of the concept you will be teaching before you will be able to effectively teach it.

Begin by prayerfully reading the SETS Method for the INDIVIDUAL found in the next chapter of this book. Then put it into practice.

I'm sure you have heard the saying 'wake up and smell the roses.' As you learn to develop having SETS in your own life, you will find that the SETS Method not only wakes you up and allows you to see that the roses exist, but it enables you to smell the fragrance and experience the beauty of the rose and all it brings into the world. You will begin to understand the love of the gardener for the bush that he tenderly planted to bring joy to each passerby. Many times we miss much of life because we do not slow down and have not trained our mind nor our eyes to see. It is imperative that we begin to live in the present moment and begin to see, really see.

When we become more sensitive to our surroundings, we become more aware of this sphere we call earth, develop gratitude and appreciation for its beauties and empathy for its creatures, and we begin to emphasize our similarities rather than our differences.

I recall driving down the street when beginning to learn the SETS Method and realized how very unaware I was of my surroundings. I was so out of touch that I had to begin with the basics such as looking at a sign and telling myself, "There is a sign," or looking at a tree and saying, "There is a tree." One morning I saw a homeless man and thought, "God loves him, too." I realized I had been journeying through life from one destination to the next in a seeming trance. That was all about to change.

I invite you to find yourself while looking for Him. C. S. Lewis, in *Mere Christianity* talks about getting ourselves out of the way so we can find Him. "The more we get what we now call 'ourselves' out of the way and let Him take us over, the more truly ourselves we become." He further explains, "... our real selves are all waiting for us in Him. It is no good trying to 'be myself' without Him. The more I resist Him and try to live on my own, the more I become dominated by my heredity and upbringing and surroundings and natural desires. In fact what I so proudly call 'Myself' becomes merely the meeting place for trains of events which I never started and which I cannot stop." He then goes on to tell us that the first step is to try to forget about the self altogether and that your real, new self, "…will come when you are looking for Him."

If you have unrelieved pains and frustrations or unfulfilled longings, perhaps, just perhaps, you are looking for something outside of Him to bring you the relief you so desperately seek. Are you missing the connection to God? And that connection, the cure for all of our ills and the ills of society, must be ingested to heal the illness. We cannot merely look at the cure and hope that the illness will by some means 'magically' go away. It will not.

You may not be able to cure society or the world, but you can take the first step by beginning with yourself right now, this very moment. Resolve to connect with God and you will see dramatic changes for good in your life, and the lives of those around you, as you develop a close, long-lasting relationship with Him.

Remember who you are. King Mufasa in the Disney film entitled *The Lion King* says the following insightful words to his young son Simba. "Simba, you have forgotten me. You have forgotten who you are and so forgotten me. Look inside yourself Simba, you are more than you have become. You must take your place in the circle of life. Remember who you are!"

One person can make a difference. This is your opportunity to begin with yourself, teach the noble child within you to connect with God, and once you have made this sacred connection, you will be able to share the music of your soul with another and begin *Teaching Children How To Connect With God*. And you will be a powerful influence for good as you teach the most important lesson you will ever teach. A lesson that will resound far into generations to come.

**ONE PERSON CAN MAKE A DIFFERENCE
BUT <u>FIRST</u> YOU MUST BEGIN WITH YOURSELF**

CHAPTER 8

SETS METHOD FOR THE INDIVIDUAL
Connect With God By Having Spiritually Enlightening Thoughts - SETS

The SETS Method is simple. It doesn't matter where you are on your ladder of spiritual progression, you can work this process and the process will work for you. Approach this experience with enthusiasm and have fun with it. <u>There are no wrong answers</u>.

Understand, you are re-training thought patterns and that takes consistency and time to gel. Don't be impatient with yourself. Remember, you will be training your mind to *recognize God's hand in all things* and to *tune in to God.*

It is important to note that for this concept to become second nature and life-changing, it must be practiced with consistency, which is the key word if you want it to make a difference in your life.

- Choose a time and area for contemplation or meditation. Make certain that you choose an area free of distractions. Yes, you must <u>turn off the television, stereo, radio, computer,</u> and choose a time when you are alone or hibernate into a secluded room or a sheltered area outside. Perhaps taking a walk will be the way you want to approach this. As long as the time and place you choose is free of distractions, any location you choose will be the correct area for you.

- Read, "NEW LIFE" (found at the end of this Chapter). Read it slowly and with softness of heart.

- Gather numerous *natural* objects (flower, leaf, stone, twig, etc). You will be relating a spiritual thought to each object, so be creative. Give your mind something to work with. Make it stretch.

- Now take a moment, look at each object, and come up with a SETS for each one, such as: for the *flower,* flowers are each unique, just as we are unique and loved by God; for the *leaf,* leaves provide shelter from the heat of the day, and so God shelters us; for the *stone,* stones come in different shapes and sizes yet each has a purpose to fulfill; for the *twig,* as the twig is bent, so grows the tree.

Remember the SETS should not be long and involved.

After a while, the process will become second nature to you, and your life will be enriched. It will be easier to live closer to God, and to know someone is to love them and SETS will help you come to know Him better. All you have to do is knock on God's door and He will open it.

- When you are ready, start choosing everyday objects such as a salt shaker, eraser, pencil, ruler, paper clip, ball, etc., and begin to associate SETS with each one. You will never run out of objects so the SETS process is nearly endless.

- Pick out objects along the way as you drive to work, to the grocery store, or to play golf, and connect SETS with them. Realize that this is <u>fun</u> and <u>exhilarating</u>. The more you believe in the process, the better, more effectively you will be able to teach it. And if you are not alone, invite everyone to join in and have **fun**. Teaching a concept is an effective learning experience not only for the student but for the teacher as well.

- You may even want to write your SETS down in a journal or a notebook that you have specifically designated as your Book of SETS (Jeffery's Book of SETS, Katie's Book of SETS, or Cathy's Book of SETS). Be sure you print 'SETS' in the left margin so that the SETS will be easily identifiable. By writing them down, your creative side will really begin to blossom.

- Note – Journal pages have been provided for you at the end of this book so that you can begin to write down your SETS.

- <u>Print</u> 'SETS' on a poster board(s) in large capital letters and place in strategic places around your home.

- It doesn't matter how old you are, read the *Chronicles of Narnia* by C. S. Lewis. These books are filled with religious symbolism. Or, since C. S. Lewis is an outstanding author, just pick up any one of his books, such as *Mere Christianity*, and start reading. Between the pages of his books is a feast for the soul.

- Take notes at church meetings. You may have very enlightening SETS when listening to a talk, sermon, or lesson.

- Experience the feeling of 'tuning in to God,' not only at church or in a beautiful setting, i.e., near nature, in the mountains, or by the ocean, but in your everyday life – that is the key. We human beings go through life seemingly with blinders on. Not looking left or right to discover the beauties and wonders all around us, but trudging forward completing our daily tasks more like robots than children of God. Begin to see, really see, and listen, allowing your awareness to be awakened.

BE CREATIVE

BE ENTHUSIASTIC

HAVE FUN

CONNECT WITH GOD AND CHANGE YOUR LIFE

Practice SETS until you are convinced of their effectiveness and have experienced a change in your life.

THEN SHARE WHAT YOU HAVE LEARNED AND

BEGIN TEACHING CHILDREN HOW TO CONNECT WITH GOD!

NEW LIFE by PAUL HARVEY
(Reprinted with permission of PAUL HARVEY NEWS)

The Rev. Harry Pritchett, Jr. is rector of All Saints Episcopal Church in Atlanta. His church includes specific ministries for the poor, for street people, and for college students. It is Pritchett who called my attention to a boy named Philip.

He was 9 -- in a Sunday School class of 8-year-olds. Eight-year-olds can be cruel. The third-graders did not welcome Philip into their group. Not just because he was older. He was "different". He suffered Down's syndrome, and its obvious manifestations: facial characteristics, slow responses, symptoms of retardation.

On the Sunday after Easter, the Sunday school teacher gathered some of those plastic eggs that pull apart in the middle – the kind in which some ladies' pantyhose are packaged. The Sunday School teacher gave one of these plastic eggs to each child. On that beautiful spring day each child was to go outdoors and discover for himself some symbol of "new life" and place that symbolic seed, leaf or whatever inside his egg. They would then open their eggs, one by one, and each youngster would explain how his find was a symbol of "new life."

So . . . The youngsters gathered 'round on the appointed day and put their eggs on a table, and the teacher began to open them. One child found a flower. All the children "oohed" and "aahed" at the lovely symbol of new life. In another was a butterfly. "Beautiful," the girls said. And it's not easy for and 8-year-old to say "beautiful." Another egg was opened to reveal a rock. Some of the children laughed. "That's crazy!" one said. "How's a rock supposed to be like a 'new life'?" Immediately a little boy spoke up and said, "That's mine. I knew everybody would get flowers and leaves and butterflies and all that stuff, so I got a rock to be different." Everyone laughed.

The teacher opened the last one and there was nothing in side. "That's not fair," someone said. "That's stupid," said another. [The] teacher felt a tug on his shirt. It was Philip. "It's mine. I did do it. It's empty. I have new life because the tomb is empty."

The class fell silent. From that day on Philip became a part of the group. They welcomed him. Whatever had made him different was never mentioned again.

Philip's family had known he would not live a long life: just too many things wrong with the tiny body. That summer, overcome by infection, Philip died. On the day of his funeral nine 8-year-old boys and girls confronted the reality of death and marched up to the altar - not with flowers.

Nine children with their Sunday School teacher placed on the casket of their friend their gift of love – an empty egg.

PART IV

TEACH WHAT YOU HAVE LEARNED

"Speak to us of Teaching . . .

If he is indeed wise he does not bid you enter the house of his wisdom,

but rather leads you to the threshold of your own mind."

Kahlil Gibran

TRUST ME

Child,

You are yet a growing bud.

Trust me,

And I will help each tender petal blossom

As a dew speckled rose

On a field of green.

I was there when you began

And nourished you beyond the veil.

Trust me now,

And when the night grows cold

My light will keep you warm

And safe from harm.

Trust me,

And though times may bring

The weight of the world

Upon your shoulders

I will help you stand erect and strong.

Trust me,

And I will take you back

Refined and purified

To that glorious field of white

Wherein you first began.

Trust me,

And I will help you blossom

Into Eternal Life.

Shanna Simpson-Christ

CHAPTER 9

PREPARING TO TEACH

Teaching a child to connect with God
is the most important lesson you will ever teach.

What teaching about SETS does for the teacher. What, you ask, will teaching about SETS do for you, as you in turn teach the concept to a child? It will continue to strengthen your connection with God, and you will become more sensitive to those things spiritual.

When you continue to see with your spiritual eyes and connect with God on a regular basis, you feel deeper, have more compassion, and others will feel the unconditional love being emitted from your heart, and your countenance will change as you act as a conduit for God's love to His children. You will begin to recognize the promptings of the spirit and will experience joy. You will understand that you are an instrument in this great Plan of God and that you have been called to further His kingdom upon the earth by teaching His children to 'come unto Him,' and you will be supremely blessed for your efforts.

When you teach, if you are thoroughly committed, have implemented the SETS Method in your own life, and taught the inner child within you, you will find that your true, divine nature will shine through. You will begin to develop a closer relationship with God and experience a peace and love far surpassing anything you have experienced before.

Trust between teacher and child. When we talk about trust between teacher and child we need to understand that children just want to be loved, accepted, and cared for. They want to be able to trust and not have that trust violated. They want to be able to resolve who you say you are with who you really are. Then, and only then, will they trust you to teach them.

Many children are walking around in this world having had to 'stuff' feelings because their trust has been betrayed. This may have happened at a very young age, therefore, in order to establish your integrity and earn their trust, you must:

- Demonstrate to the child that there is a consistency between who you are and who you say you are.
- Demonstrate that what you teach is in harmony with what you believe deep down inside yourself.

So take a moment and go to your quiet place, away from distractions. Maybe it's a drive in the mountains or by the sea, a walk in the woods, or just sitting peacefully in a nearby park. If you can find a place where there are pine trees you will be doubly rewarded. There is something very special about the energy of the pine tree.

To enable you to develop teacher/student trust, you need to ask yourself these questions and evaluate where you are:

- Is who I say am consistent with who I really am inside?
- Is what I teach in harmony with what I truly believe?

It is very important at this point to have a good understanding of your honesty with yourself, and if you are not in harmony, bring yourself back into harmony. TO THINE OWN SELF BE TRUE.

You cannot effect behavioral change in a child until he or she feels acceptance, love, and trust; and we must learn to trust the Master Teacher.

Preparing to teach. Forget the idea that you have to be a spiritual giant to teach the Spiritually Enlightening Thoughts (**SETS**) Method, or to have studied in the spiritual academy for all things great and wonderful. You absolutely do not. You just have to be a person who says, "I want to be able to teach the children to draw closer to God by connecting with Him on a regular basis, and to teach them to recognize His voice when He speaks to them. I want to be able to help them understand their purpose in this uncertain world and to provide a way for them to experience the ultimate joy and peace that comes to those who live their lives close to God."

Now that you have learned the concept you will be teaching, look at yourself as the child's 'guide to God.' You want them to learn to 'tune in to God,' and in order to do this you need to prepare yourself by doing the following:

- Prayerfully ask God to bless you with the faith, understanding, and commitment to enable you to teach the SETS Method effectively. This book is merely a guide.

- If you are instructing in a classroom setting, think about each of the children you will be teaching and consider that for some this may be one of the first opportunities they will have to openly express their feelings in a safe, non-threatening atmosphere, since not all homes are ideal and supportive.

- <u>Read to understand</u> the SETS Method Teaching Modules in Chapter Ten and Chapter Eleven.

- Commit to God and to yourself that you will continue teaching SETS as often as necessary (a <u>minimum</u> of once a week) until the SETS Method becomes second nature to the child. Understand this is not a 'quick fix.'

Johann von Goethe offers us the following insight:
" In the realm of ideas everything depends on enthusiasm;
in the real world, all rests on perseverance."

The SETS Method is beautifully simple and simply beautiful. You will be training thought patterns to relate everyday objects with spiritual concepts, thereby training the mind to think **S**piritually **E**nlightening **T**hought**s** (**SETS**), and in doing so you will be teaching children how to connect with God. It is important to note once again that thoughts precede actions and wholesome, God-based thoughts produce wholesome, God-based actions.

To follow are two Teaching Modules, each one providing detailed steps necessary to teach the SETS Method:

For the FAMILY
For the CLASSROOM

Identify the Module that will fit the needs of those you will be teaching and prayerfully **read to understand**.

NOW LET US BEGIN *TEACHING CHILDREN HOW TO CONNECT WITH GOD!*

CHAPTER 10

SETS METHOD FOR THE FAMILY

Teach Children To Connect With God By Having
Spiritually Enlightening Thoughts - SETS

IT'S SIMPLE AND FUN! IT NEEDS TO BE PRACTICED WITH CONSISTENCY, OVER TIME, WITH LOVING SUPPORT IN A NON-JUDGMENTAL ENVIRONMENT.

BE CREATIVE AND PRAYERFUL IN DECIDING HOW TO PRESENT THE INFORMATION. REMEMBER, YOU ARE TEACHING A CONCEPT THAT WILL BE LIFE-CHANGING.

Teaching the SETS Method in a family setting is similar to the classroom setting, with a few subtle changes.

Teaching children to connect with God is a process that takes time to gel. Remember, you will be training the mind to *recognize God's hand in all things* and teaching them to *tune in to God*.

It is important to note that for this concept to become second nature to your child and be life-changing , it must be practiced <u>consistently at a minimum of once a week</u>. Consistency is the key word if you want to make a difference in their lives.

The idea is to make it fun for them. Even though the concept is simple, it will be more difficult for some to understand than others. Be patient. <u>There are no wrong answers</u>. Understand, you are re-training thought patterns, and that takes consistency and time.

- PREPARE: Prior to the time when you will present the SETS for the first time, go outside and gather enough *natural* objects (flower, leaf, stone, twig, etc.) so that each participant will have one. Now take a moment, look at each object and, come up with a SETS for each one, such as: for the *flower,* the flower is delicate just like many of God's creations; for the *leaf,* as leaves blow in the wind, so do we if we are not anchored in Christ; for the *stone,* as the stone can be tumbled by the winds of adversity and become smooth and perfected, so can we; for the *twig,* although a twig may be twisted and bent, it still has a purpose to fulfill.
Remember the SETS should not be long and involved.
- TIME NEEDED: Gather your family around. In planning this exercise, in the beginning, allow 2 to 3 minutes per person. The more familiar they become with the SETS Method, the faster they will be able to come up with a thought.
- TEACHING AREA: Make certain that the room is free of distractions. That means <u>turn off the television, stereo, radio, and computers</u>. The family needs to have total focus on what they are doing. It may not be easy for them at first, but the more they practice, the easier it will become.
- YOUR DEMEANOR: Maintain a soft voice throughout the exercise. Your family should not at any time feel threatened or embarrassed for not being able to come up with an answer. Assure them that it will be easier the more they practice and that they need to provide mutual support for each other.

1. INTRODUCING THE SETS METHOD FOR THE FIRST TIME:

It is important to build the SETS Method on a solid foundation. Tell them that you will be using objects that they see all the time to help them connect with God. Explain that they are to look at the object and relate a spiritual thought to it. Show an object and give an example. Tell them you are going to call this process **Spiritually Enlightening Thoughts (SETS).**

<u>Print</u> 'SETS' on a poster board in large capital letters. Save this to use every time you teach about SETS. Make sure you display it every time.

Explain that after a while the process will become second nature to them, that their lives will be enriched as they live closer to God. Help them to understand that to know someone is to love them and that SETS will help them to know God better.

Remember, adults as well as children should participate. If the adults don't participate, this sends a message to the children that what is being taught is not important.

a. Read "NEW LIFE" to your family (found at the end of Chapter Eight). This will, by example, provide another powerful way to introduce the concept. Read it slowly and with feeling. It helps if you have read it prior to presenting it to your family, so you have the idea of the story. You may want to have a discussion about its meaning after you have read it to them.

b. Give each person an object that you have collected and tell them that you are going to give them a couple of quiet moments to think of **S**piritually **E**nlightening **T**hought**s** **(SETS)** for the object they have. Give them two or three more examples so they get the idea. Discourage talking. They need to be prayerful and meditative to allow their minds to become familiar with this way of thought. Emphasize that <u>there are no wrong answers</u>. This sends two messages, one that it is a safe environment, and two that they are not to judge each other's answers but be supportive.

c. At this point decide what works best for your family. You can either begin at one end of the room and, one-by-one, ask each family member for the SETS they thought of, or ask for volunteers as to who will be first. Evaluate your family and see which will work best and will be the most non-threatening. Maintain gentle control so that they provide loving support, not judgment or criticism, for each other. One disrespectful comment can undermine everything you are trying to do.

d. After everyone has had a chance to participate, thank them. Tell them how well they did and assure them it will get easier the more they practice.

IF AN INDIVIDUAL CANNOT THINK OF AN ANSWER: Tell them that it's okay and that next time will be easier. It is very important that <u>before</u> you move to the next person for their thought, <u>you</u> provide SETS for the object of the person who could not think of an answer.

AT THE END OF YOUR TIME TOGETHER: Remind them to look for SETS during the week. Tell them how much fun you had and that your family will be doing this again next week at breakfast, dinner, etc. Whenever it works for your family.

2. THE SECOND TIME YOU TEACH SETS AND THEREAFTER:

a. Provide an environment that is free of distractions. That means <u>turn off the television, stereo, radio, and computers</u>. The family needs to have total focus on what they are doing.

Provide an environment free of distractions.

b. Put the poster board with the word 'SETS' printed on it in a conspicuous place in the room.

Put poster board with 'SETS' on it in conspicuous place.

c. Briefly remind your family what SETS are.
In your own words, reinforce the idea that this is going to be a 'fun' experience and that it will get easier the more they practice, that their lives will be enriched, and they will begin to live closer to God. Help them understand that to know someone is to love them and that SETS will help them to know God better. Remind them that all they have to do is knock on God's door and He will open it.
Give an example. Share an experience <u>you</u> have had as you practiced having SETS the past week. Be enthusiastic.

Remind them what SETS are.

Explain this will be a fun experience and that they will begin to live closer to God.

Give an example.

d. Ask <u>them</u> to share any experiences they may have had during the week as they practiced having SETS. This is a very important part of the SETS learning experience. You will have more participation with this as time goes on, once they become familiar with the thought process of SETS.
Don't apply any pressure or make them feel that something is wrong if they didn't think of SETS that week or don't have SETS to share. <u>Do not go around the room asking each to</u>

Ask them to share a SET experience.

Be encouraging.

<u>share</u>. This part of the SETS process needs to be voluntary. Everyone will arrive at this point of sharing at a different time.

e. For the first few weeks, use the same objects as the week before, asking each family member to choose an object they had not chosen prior. Then, as before, give them a few quiet moments, free of distraction, to think of SETS for the object they have chosen.

Choose objects.

The first objects you use should be from nature. It will be easier for them to associate SETS with natural objects that they consider to be made by God.

Use your own judgment. As the weeks pass and it becomes easier for the children, begin using everyday objects such as a salt shaker, eraser, pencil, ruler, paper clip, ball, etc. (photographs, pictures, or drawings work well also). You may even want to go to the local party supply store and get some little inexpensive trinkets to use in the exercise. Then allow them to keep the items in their room as a reminder of SETS. Remember, BE CREATIVE and BE PREPARED with an answer for each object.

As you continue in the SETS learning process, invite the children to look for objects on their own to share.

Invite them to look for objects.

f. After they have chosen their object, give them one or two quiet moments, free of distractions, to think of a SET.

Provide quiet time, free of distractions.

g. Remind them that there are <u>no wrong answers</u>. Promote an atmosphere of love and support.

No wrong answers.

h. Ask them to share their SETS by either beginning at one end of the room and working your way around it or asking for volunteers, whichever way works best for your family. Make sure

Ask them to share their SETS.

you provide an opportunity for everyone to share their SETS, **adults and children alike.**

i. If an individual can't think of an answer, reassure them with love that it is okay and that the next time will be easier. Remember, it is very important that <u>before</u> you move on to the next person for their thought, <u>you</u> provide SETS for the person who could not think of an answer. Keep in mind that this must be done in a loving, non-judgmental manner.

Reassure them if they can't think of an answer.

You provide SETS.

j. After everyone has had a chance to participate, thank them. Tell them how well they did and assure them it will get easier the more they practice.

Thank them.

k. Invite them to practice SETS during the week by looking at everyday objects and connecting a spiritual thought with them.

Invite them to look for SETS during the week.

BE CREATIVE

MAKE IT FUN

TEACH THE SETS METHOD A <u>MINIMUM</u> OF ONCE A WEEK

3. AFTER YOU HAVE TAUGHT THE SETS METHOD FOR A WHILE, HERE ARE ADDITIONAL SUGGESTIONS YOU MAY WANT TO TRY:

a. Ask them to teach what they have learned to their grandma, grandpa, nieces, nephews, aunts, uncles, or friends.

b. Use the SETS idea to play a game in the car when you travel. Just ask them to pick out an object along the side of the road and relate SETS to it. There are all kinds of fun things along the side of the road that they can use. This is very creative, a lot of fun, and a very effective way to learn to train the mind to see SETS. And what is even better, everyone in the car can participate. A great family activity.

c. Invite them to write down the SETS they have thought of either in their journal or in a notebook that they have specifically designated as their book of SETS (Andrea's Book of SETS, Troy's Book of SETS, or Kerri's Book of SETS). You may even want to give each family member their own book of SETS to write in, and make sure you include a pen. You can get very creative with this idea.

Suggest that they print the letters 'SETS' in the left margin if they are writing them in their journal. That will indicate to them which entries are SETS so they can find them easily.

By printing the letters 'SETS' in the left margin, they will be able to identify the SETS if they need them for talks or to give themselves a boost when life gets a little rough.

By writing them down, their creative side will really begin to blossom, and it will be fun for them to look back at what they have written.

Note – Journal pages have been provided for you at the end of this book so that you can begin to keep a record of SETS

d. Invite them to take notes at church meetings. They may have very enlightening SETS when they are listening to a talk, sermon, or a lesson.

e. Here is an idea if your children love to read – C. S. Lewis has written an enchanting series of books entitled *The Chronicles Of Narnia.* Contained within the pages of the books is a lot of religious symbolism. As a family, you may want to read these books then discuss the symbolism contained therein.

C. S. Lewis had the capacity to write a wonderful story and the reader, depending on their depth of understanding of 'those things spiritual,' will be served up a portion equal to that understanding. The more spiritual knowledge you have with which to relate, the more you will understand. It is a beautiful concept that God uses as well.

The more we know, the more we understand; and the more we understand, the more our eyes are opened to knowledge, line upon line, precept upon precept.

USE THIS METHOD IN *TEACHING CHILDREN HOW TO CONNECT WITH GOD* AND YOU WILL CHANGE THEIR LIVES

CHAPTER 11

SETS METHOD FOR THE CLASSROOM

Teach Children To Connect With God By Having
Spiritually Enlightening Thoughts - SETS

IT'S SIMPLE AND FUN! IT NEEDS TO BE PRACTICED WITH CONSISTENCY, OVER TIME, WITH LOVING SUPPORT IN A NON-JUDGMENTAL ENVIRONMENT.

BE CREATIVE AND PRAYERFUL IN DECIDING HOW TO PRESENT THE INFORMATION. REMEMBER, YOU ARE TEACHING A CONCEPT THAT WILL BE LIFE-CHANGING.

Teaching children to connect with God is a process that takes time to gel. Remember, you will be training the mind to *recognize God's hand in all things* and teaching them to *tune in to God*.

It is important to note that for this concept to become second nature to the child and be life-changing, it must be practiced <u>consistently at a minimum of once a week</u>. Consistency is the key word if you want to make a difference in their lives. These sessions will be Mini Teaching Moments and will not take the entire class time, except perhaps the first lesson where you will introduce the concept of **S**piritually **E**nlightening **T**hought**s** (**SETS**).

The idea is to make it fun for them. Even though the concept is simple, it will be more diffi-cult for some to understand than others. Be patient. <u>There are no wrong answers</u>. Understand, you are re-training thought patterns and that takes consistency and time.

- PREPARE: Prior to the time when you will present SETS for the first time, go outside and gather enough *natural* objects (flower, leaf, stone, twig, etc.) so that each participant will have one. Now take a moment, look at each object and come up with a SETS for each one, such as: for the *flower*, each petal is important to the flower and we are each impor-tant to God; for the *leaf*, the leaves seem to reach toward the light and we should reach toward His light; for the *stone*, stones can line the path to God; for the *twig*, we can use the twig to point the way to God.
Remember the SETS should not be long and involved.
- TIME NEEDED: In planning this exercise, in the beginning, allow a minimum 2 to 3 minutes per child. The more familiar they become with the SETS Method, the faster they will be able to come up with a thought.
- TEACHING AREA: Make certain that the teaching area is free of distractions. The group needs to have total focus on what they are doing. It may not be easy for them at first. The more they practice, the easier it will become.
- YOUR DEMEANOR: Maintain a soft voice throughout the exercise. They should not at any time feel threatened or embarrassed for not being able to come up with an answer. Assure them that it will be easier the more they practice and that they need to provide mutual support for each other.
- BEGINNING OF CLASS: This exercise is best done at the <u>beginning</u> of class <u>each week</u>. By putting it at the beginning, you are making a statement that it is important; therefore, you are going to make certain that you have enough time to complete the exercise. If you put it at the end, you may run out of time and not everyone will get a turn to participate. It is imperative that everyone has the opportunity to share their SETS or those that do not may leave the class feeling unfulfilled.

1. INTRODUCING THE SETS METHOD FOR THE FIRST TIME:

It is important to build the SETS Method on a solid foundation. Tell them that you will be using objects that they see all the time to help them connect with God. Explain that they are to look at the object and relate a spiritual thought to it. Show an object and give an example. Tell them you are going to call this process **Spiritually Enlightening Thoughts (SETS).**

<u>Print</u> 'SETS' on the chalkboard or poster board in large capital letters.

Explain that after a while the process will become second nature to them, that their lives will be enriched as they live closer to God. Help them to understand that to know someone is to love them and that SETS will help them know God better.

a. Read, "NEW LIFE" to the class (found at the end of Chapter Eight). This will, by example, provide another powerful way to introduce the concept. Read it slowly and with feeling.

b. Give each person one of the objects you collected prior to class and tell them that you are going to give them a couple of quiet moments to think of **Spiritually Enlightening Thoughts (SETS)** for the object they have. Give them two or three more examples so they get the idea. Discourage talking. They need to be prayerful and meditative to allow their mind to become familiar with this way of thought. Emphasize that <u>there are no wrong answers</u>. This sends two messages, one that it is a safe environment, and two that they are not to judge each other's answers but be supportive.

c. At this point decide what works best for your class. You can either begin at one end of the room and, one-by-one, ask each youth for the SETS they thought of, or ask for volunteers as to who will be first. Evaluate your group and see which will work best and will be the most non-threatening.

Maintain gentle control of the class so that they provide loving support, not judgment or criticism, for each other. One disrespectful comment can undermine everything you are trying to do.

d. After everyone has had a chance to participate, thank them. Tell them how well they did and assure them it will get easier the more they practice.

IF AN INDIVIDUAL CANNOT THINK OF AN ANSWER: Tell them that it's okay and that next time will be easier. It is very important that <u>before</u> you move to the next person for their thought, <u>you</u> provide SETS for the object of the person who could not think of an answer.

AT THE END OF CLASS: Leave one or two minutes to reinforce the concept of SETS at the end of <u>each</u> class to remind them of what they learned that day. Be brief.

2. THE SECOND TIME YOU TEACH SETS AND THEREAFTER:

a. AT THE <u>BEGINNING</u> OF <u>EVERY</u> CLASS <u>print</u> 'SETS' on the chalkboard or on a large poster board.

Print 'SETS' on the board.

b. In your own words, briefly and concisely explain what SETS are, for those who are new or those who may not have understood or had a problem participating before.

Explain what SETS are.

In your own words, reinforce the idea that it is going to be a 'fun' experience and that it will get easier the more they practice, that their lives will be enriched, and they will begin to live closer to God. Help them understand that to know someone is to love them and that SETS will help them to know God better. Remind them that all they have to do is knock on God's door and He will open it.

Explain this will be a fun experience and that they will begin to live closer to God.

Give an example. Share an experience <u>you</u> have had as you practiced having SETS the past week. Be enthusiastic.

Give an example.

c. Ask <u>them</u> to share any experiences they may have had during the week as they practiced having SETS. This is a very important part of the SETS learning experience. You will have more participation with this as time goes on, once they become familiar with the thought process of SETS.

Ask them to share a SET experience.

Don't apply any pressure or make them feel that something is wrong if they didn't think of SETS that week or don't have SETS to share. <u>Do not go around the class asking each to share.</u> This part of the SETS program needs to be voluntary. Everyone will arrive at this point of sharing at a different time.

Be encouraging.

d. For the first few weeks, use the same objects as the week before, asking each member of the group to choose an object they had not chosen prior.

Choose objects.

Then, as before, give them a few quiet moments, free of distraction, to think of SETS for the object they have chosen. The first objects you use should be from nature. It will be easier for them to associate SETS with natural objects that they consider to be made by God.

Use your own judgment. As the weeks pass and it becomes easier for the class, bring everyday objects such as a salt shaker, eraser, pencil, ruler, paper clip, ball, etc. (photographs, pictures, or drawings work well also). Once I even went to the local party supply house and bought little inexpensive plastic trinkets to use in class. Then I let the children take them home as a reminder. BE CREATIVE and BE PREPARED with an answer for each object.

As you continue in the SETS learning process, invite the children to look for objects to bring to class.

Invite them to look for objects.

e. After they have chosen their object, give them one or two quiet moments, free of distractions, to think of a SET.

Provide quiet time, free of distractions.

f. Remind them that there are <u>no wrong answers</u>. Promote an atmosphere of love and support.

No wrong answers.

g. Ask them to share the SETS they thought of by either beginning at one end of the room and working your way around it or asking for volunteers, whichever way works best for your class. Make sure you provide an opportunity for everyone to share their SETS.

Ask them to share their SETS.

h. As we talked about before, if an individual can't think of an answer, reassure them with love that it is okay and that the next time will be easier.

Reassure them if they can't think of an answer.

Remember, it is very important that <u>before</u> you move on to the next person for their thought, <u>you</u> provide SETS for the person who could not think of an answer. Keep in mind, that this must be done in a loving, non-judgmental manner.

You provide SETS.

i. After everyone has had a chance to participate, thank them. Tell them how well they did and assure them it will get easier the more they practice.

Thank them.

j. Invite them to practice SETS during the week by looking at everyday objects and connecting a spiritual thought with them.

Invite them to look for SETS during the week.

k. AT THE END OF <u>EVERY</u> CLASS: Allow one to two minutes to reinforce the concept of SETS. Be brief.

Reinforce SETS concept at end of class.

BE CREATIVE

MAKE IT FUN

TEACH THE SETS METHOD A <u>MINIMUM</u> OF ONCE A WEEK

3. AFTER YOU HAVE TAUGHT THE SETS METHOD FOR AWHILE, HERE ARE ADDITIONAL IDEAS YOU MAY WANT TO SUGGEST:

a. Ask them to teach what they have learned to their brothers, sisters, grandmothers, and grandfathers (teaching mom and dad would be okay too).

b. Suggest that they play a SETS game in the car when they travel. They just pick out an object along the side of the road and relate SETS to it. There are all kinds of fun things along the side of the road that they can use. This is very creative, a lot of fun, and a very effective way to learn to train the mind to see SETS. And what is even better, everyone in the car can participate. A great family activity.

c. Invite them to write down the SETS they have thought of either in their journal or in a notebook that they have specifically designated as their Book of SETS (Kennedy's Book of SETS, Whitney's Book of SETS, or Trevor's Book of SETS). Suggest that they print the letters 'SETS' in the left margin if they are writing them in their journal. That will indicate to them which entries are SETS so they can find them easily.

By printing the letters 'SETS' in the left margin, they will be able to identify the SETS if they need them for talks or to give themselves a boost when life gets a little rough.

By writing them down, their creative side will really begin to blossom, and it will be fun for them to look back at what they have written.

Note – Journal pages have been provided for you at the end of this book so that you can begin to keep a record of SETS

d. Ask if your class can teach some of the younger classes about SETS. Teaching is an effective learning experience not only for the student but for the teacher as well.

e. Invite them to take notes at church meetings. They may have very enlightening SETS when they are listening to a talk, sermon, or a lesson.

Here is an idea if the children in your class love to read – C. S. Lewis has written an enchanting series of books entitled *The Chronicles Of Narnia*. Contained within the pages of the books is a lot of religious symbolism. As an outside activity or perhaps in class, you may want to read these books then discuss the symbolism.

C. S. Lewis had the capacity to write a wonderful story and the reader, depending on their depth of understanding of 'those things spiritual,' will be served up a portion equal to that understanding. The more spiritual knowledge you have with which to relate, the more you will understand. This is a beautiful concept that God uses as well.

The more we know, the more we understand; and the more we understand, the more our eyes are opened to knowledge; thus, we are added upon, line upon line, precept upon precept.

USE THIS METHOD IN *TEACHING CHILDREN HOW TO CONNECT WITH GOD* AND YOU WILL CHANGE THEIR LIVES

PART V

WHERE DO WE GO FROM HERE?

"Light tomorrow with today."

Elizabeth Barrett Browning

"Happiness does not depend on outward things, but the way we see them."
Leo Tolstoy

CHAPTER 12

LET ME HEAR FROM YOU

www.SETSconnection.com

Congratulations! You have accomplished a great deal as you have pondered, prayed, and practiced connecting with Him by the sacred observance of His creations. You recognize that this earth life is challenging at best, but you have experienced comfort and understanding as you have felt God's unconditional love for you.

SETS have empowered you to once again see the majesty in the world around you. The child within you has been allowed to come through and reach out to all things beautiful. Your spiritual eyes have been opened and invited you to see, to feel, to experience the palette of life painted in brilliant hues of color. You have had a renewal of spirit.

You began with yourself and learned that when you again saw life as a child, the wonders were still there, all around, just waiting to be rediscovered, all you had to do was look.

Your whole world opened up full of grandeur and fascination, and it bid you to explore and to learn, and invited your senses to participate. You have seen the glorious sights of discovery, felt the warmth of the breeze against your cheek, and perhaps even heard the call of a lark, a cricket's chatter, the croaking of a frog, or the howl of a coyote on a cold winter night. And you have learned that awareness leads to discovery.

You have become more sensitive to the touch of a loved one's hand in comfort. As you stroked your pet's back, you felt the love and the bond that has developed between you over the years. You have learned that placed before you is the palette of life on which <u>you</u> choose the colors and understand that <u>you</u> have been invited to paint the painting of your life. For it is there, just waiting to be painted, and it can only be painted by you. It's your painting, your story. And you have learned to connect with God so that you can paint it.

You have taught of God's unconditional love for each of His children. You have the understanding that all children, and the noble child that lives within you, have been endowed with magnificent gifts of the spirit and have great future potential.

As you have acted as the conduit for God's love, you taught the most important lessons you will ever teach. Lessons that will resound into generations to come, and you have been a powerful influence for good as you, in partnership with God, have been *Teaching Children How To Connect With God.*

What a magnificent journey you have been on. You have done so well and have so much to share that I would like to extend this special invitation to you.

 *YOUR PERSONAL INVITATION* 

As one who has practiced and/or taught the SETS Method, you are invited to contribute your faith-promoting SETS experiences for possible inclusion in future books that are right now on the 'drawing board.'

Just practice the SETS Method for a minimum of three (3) months for the INDIVIDUAL or six (6) months in a FAMILY or CLASSROOM setting. Then let me hear from you by going to my website at www.SETSconnection.com and sharing your faith-promoting SETS experiences. The two categories we are looking for are:

    a.   Profound, faith-promoting examples of SETS.
           and

    b.   How practicing the SETS Method has changed your life or the lives of those you have taught.

If your writing is chosen, it may be included in future books that will incorporate individual, personal experiences of those who have practiced and/or taught the SETS Method.

I look forward to hearing from you!

An old Chinese proverb says, **"The journey of a thousand miles must begin with a single step."**

May God be with you and bless you on your journey.

The Beginning . . .

PART VI

YOUR SETS JOURNAL

"The happiest man is he who learns from nature the lessons of worship."
Ralph Waldo Emerson

_________________________________ **SETS JOURNAL**

Your name

Record your SETS on the journal pages that follow. Try printing a word on the line in the left margin as a reminder of the specific SETS you are writing about.

ABOUT THE AUTHOR

PERSONALLY SPEAKING

Shirley Hildreth first developed and taught the SETS Method nearly ten years ago and has seen the life-changing, long-lasting, positive results it has had on those she taught.

A strong commitment to write about *SETS* lead her to enroll in writing classes and intellectual property law classes at the University of Nevada – Las Vegas; participate in many writers' workshops through Ambassador University, which provided valuable instruction in non-fiction writing, marketing, and publishing.

Shirley has a well-established business management and marketing background, been appointed to numerous boards and committees in her community, and was awarded the Clark County Proclamation of Service Award for being an "outstanding citizen who has contributed greatly to our community".

As Sales Manager Nevada's largest commercial real estate brokerage, she wrote and published the Annual Southern Nevada Economic Report, developed marketing programs, and represented her firm in training and speaking engagements. She was also Vice President of development and property management firms with holdings in six states, and President of a mortgage-banking firm that was formed to provide funding for corporate holdings.

On a more personal note ~ Shirley has raised children, flown planes, crashed computers, painted paintings, taught classes to both adults and youth, photographed many spectacular scenes, amazing animals, and beloved people; and music continues to play an important role in her life.

And her love of writing has launched her on one of the most magnificent journeys of her life. What compelled Shirley to begin this journey you ask? The answer is God!

<u>**WATCH FOR**</u>

The second book, ***SETS - Musings Of The Spirit*** – a collection of inspirational parables and stories written by the author to further reinforce the SETS Method taught in *SETS Teaching Children How To Connect With God* and awaken the readers understanding of how SETS can be implemented in their life. Projected publishing date of Spring, 2004.

The third book in the SETS series, ***SETS - I Know You're There!*** a book written for children to teach them, through the gentle observance of God's creations, of His unconditional love for them. The principles taught in this heartwarming book are based on the SETS Method outlined in *SETS Teaching Children How To Connect With God.* - Projected publishing dated of Christmas, 2004.

The fourth book, ***SETS - A Glimpse Of Heaven***, a compilation from responses of readers based on experiences and insights gained from their implementation of the SETS Method.

To receive advanced notice when these books become available, please e-mail: publisher@MUSEimagery.com **OR   fax your request to: 702-233-1762**

Make certain you include your **name, address, e-mail address, phone number** and specify that you want to be placed on the ADVANCED BOOK INFORMATION mailing list.

<u>**MEDIA KIT**</u>

The author's Media Kit can be downloaded on the publisher's website at www.MUSEimagery.com   **OR   contact the publisher.**

<u>**PUBLISHER**</u>

Muse Imagery
9811 W. Charleston Blvd., Suite 2390
Las Vegas, NV 89117-7519
Phone   702-233-5910
Fax   702-233-1762
E-mail publisher@MUSEimagery.com

<u>**ORDER BOOK**</u>

Order autographed copies of *SETS Teaching Children How To Connect With God* by:
Ordering directly from the author's website www.SETSconnection.com OR
Faxing or mailing the Order Form on the next page.

Ask for ***SETS Teaching Children How To Connect With God*** at your favorite bookstore.

QUICK ORDER FORM
SETS TEACHING CHILDREN HOW TO CONNECT WITH GOD

NAME _________________________________ DATE ___________________________

ADDRESS ____

____

CITY _______________________ STATE _________________ ZIP ________________

PHONE (_____)_________________ E-MAIL ADDRESS __________________________

_______ **NUMBER OF BOOKS ORDERED**

Price for each book - $19.95 plus a shipping and handling fee of $4.00 for the first book plus $2.00 for each additional book.

Sales Tax: Nevada Residents add $1.50 sales tax (7.5%)

Payment:　　__ **Check**　　　　__ **Credit card**

　　　　　　　　__ **VISA**　　　　__ **MASTER CARD**　　　　__ **DISCOVER**

Credit Card No. ____

Name on Card ___________________________________ **Exp. Date** _________

FAX ORDER - <u>Print this page</u>, complete information and fax to: 702-233-1762

MAIL ORDER - <u>Print this page</u>, complete information and mail it to:

> Muse Imagery
> 9811 W. Charleston Blvd. Suite 2390
> Las Vegas, NV 89117-7519

If paying by check – *make your check out to* ***Muse Imagery.***

__ **Add autographed personalization:**

To: ____

Brief Message: ____

____

If you have questions about your order please contact the <u>orderdesk@SETSconnection.com</u>.

Visit our website at <u>www.SETSconnection.com</u>

THANK YOU FOR YOUR ORDER

Printed in the United States
1363600001B/155-466